Factual writing: exploring and challenging social reality

J.R. Martin

Series Editor: Frances Christie

Oxford University Press
1989

Oxford University Press
Walton Street, Oxford OX2 6DP

Oxford   New York   Toronto
Delhi   Bombay   Calcutta   Madras   Karachi
Petaling Jaya   Singapore   Hong Kong   Tokyo
Nairobi   Dar es Salaam   Cape Town
Melbourne   Auckland

and associated companies in
Berlin   Ibadan

Oxford English and the *Oxford English* logo are trade marks of
Oxford University Press

ISBN 019 437158 1

Printed in Hong Kong.

About the author

J. R. Martin

Jim Martin is currently a Senior Lecturer in the Department of Linguistics at the University of Sydney. His main interest is in the way in which people put sentences together into texts that are coherent and appropriate to their context. In developing his ideas he has worked mainly on the spoken and written language of children and the spoken language of schizophrenic speakers. English and Tagalog (Pilipino) are the languages he is trying to understand from this point of view.

As far as theory is concerned, he is a systemic-functional linguist, trying to make use of and develop ideas taken from Firth, Halliday, and Hjelmslev. With respect to applications, he has been working since his undergraduate days in Toronto with teachers and students, principally in primary schools. He hopes to be able to develop a way of looking at language that will be useful and relevant in education.

He helped Sherry Rochester write a book on schizophrenic discourse in 1979—*Crazy Talk* (Plenum, New York) and edited a collection of disappearing papers on systemic linguistics with Michael Halliday in 1981—*Reading in Systemic Linguistics* (Batsford, London). In 1983 he wrote a general introduction to his ideas about relating language to context, 'Language, register and genre', for inclusion in the Deakin BEd coursebook ECT418 *Children Writing: Reader*.

Foreword

In a sense, educational interest in language is not new. Studies of rhetoric and of grammar go back as far as the Greeks; in the English-speaking countries, studies of the classical languages, and more recently of English itself, have had a well established place in educational practice. Moreover, a number of the issues which have aroused the most passionate debates about how to develop language abilities have tended to remain, resurfacing at various points in history in somewhat different formulations perhaps, but nonetheless still there, and still lively.

Of these issues, probably the most lively has been that concerning the extent to which explicit knowledge about language on the part of the learner is a desirable or a useful thing. But the manner in which discussion about this issue has been conducted has often been allowed to obscure other and bigger questions: questions, for example, both about the nature of language as an aspect of human experience, and about language as a resource of fundamental importance in the building of human experience. The tendency in much of the western intellectual tradition has been to dissociate language and experience, in such a way that language is seen as rather neutral, merely serving to 'carry' the fruits of experience. Whereas in this view language is seen as a kind of 'conduit', subservient to experience in various ways, an alternative view, as propounded in the books in this series, would argue that language is itself not only a part of experience, but intimately involved in the manner in which we construct and organise experience. As such, it is never neutral, but deeply implicated in building meaning. One's notions concerning how to teach about language will differ quite markedly, depending upon the view one adopts concerning language and experience. In fact, though discussions concerning teaching about language can sometimes be interesting, in practice many such discussions have proved theoretically ill-founded and barren, serving merely to perpetuate a number of unhelpful myths about language.

The most serious and confusing of these myths are those which would suggest we can dissociate language from meaning — form from function, or form from 'content'. Where such myths apply, teaching about language becomes a matter of teaching about 'language rules' — normally grammatical rules — and as history has demonstrated over the years, such teaching rapidly degenerates into the arid pursuit of parts of speech and the parsing of isolated sentences. Meaning, and the critical role of language in the building of meaning, are simply overlooked, and the kinds of knowledge about language made available to the learner are of a very limited kind.

The volumes in this series of monographs devoted to language education in my view provide a much better basis upon which to address questions related to the teaching about language than has been the case anywhere in the English-speaking world for some time now. I make this claim for several reasons, one of the most important being that the series never sought directly to establish a model for teaching about language at all. On the contrary, it sought to establish a principled model of language, which, once properly articulated, allows us to address many questions of an educational nature, including those to do with teaching about language. To use Halliday's term (1978), such a model sees language primarily as a 'social semiotic', and as a resource for meaning, centrally involved in the processes by which human beings negotiate, construct and change the nature of social experience. While the series certainly does not claim to have had the last word on these and related subjects, I believe it does do much to set a new educational agenda — one which enables us to look closely at the role of language both in living and in learning: one which, moreover, provides a basis upon which to decide those kinds of teaching and learning about language which may make a legitimate contribution to the development of the learner.

I have said that arguments to do with teaching about language have been around for a long time: certainly as long as the two hundred years of white settlement in Australia. In fact, coincidentally, just as the first settlers were taking up their enforced residence in the Australian colony of New South Wales, Lindley Murray was preparing his *English Grammar* (1795), which, though not the only volume produced on the subject in the eighteenth century, was certainly the best. Hundreds of school grammars that were to appear in Britain and Australia for the next century at least, were to draw very heavily upon what Murray had written. The parts of speech, parsing and sentence analysis, the latter as propounded by Morell (an influential inspector of schools in England), were the principal elements in the teaching about language in the Australian colonies, much as they were in England throughout the century. By the 1860s and 1870s the Professor of Classics and Logic at Sydney University, Charles Badham, who had arrived from England in 1867, publicly disagreed with the examining authorities in New South Wales concerning the teaching of grammar. To the contemporary reader there is a surprising modernity about many of his objections, most notably his strongly held conviction that successful control of one's language is learned less as a matter of committing to memory the parts of speech and the principles of parsing, than as a matter of frequent opportunity for use.

Historically, the study by which issues of use had been most effectively addressed had been that of rhetoric, in itself quite old in the English-speaking tradition, dating back at least to the sixteenth century. Rhetorical studies flourished in the eighteenth century, the best known works on the subject being George Campbell's *The Philosophy of Rhetoric* (1776), and Hugh Blair's *Lectures on Rhetoric and Belles Lettres* (1783), while in the nineteenth century Richard Whately published his work, *Elements of Rhetoric* (1828). As the nineteenth century proceeded, scholarly work on rhetoric declined, as was testified by the markedly inferior but nonetheless influential works of Alexander Bain (*English Composition and Rhetoric*, 1866; Revised version, 1887). Bain, in fact, did much to corrupt and destroy the older rhetorical traditions, primarily because he lost sight of the need for a basic concern with meaning in language. Bain's was the century of romanticism after all: on the one hand, Matthew Arnold was extolling the civilising influence of English literature in the development of children; on the other hand, there was a tendency towards suspicion, even contempt, for those who wanted to take a scholarly look at the linguistic organisation of texts, and at the ways in which they were structured for the building of meaning. In 1921, Ballard (who was an expert witness before the Newbolt Enquiry on the teaching of English), wrote a book called *Teaching the Mother Tongue*, in which he noted among other things, that unfortunately in England at least rhetorical studies had become associated with what were thought to be rather shallow devices for persuasion and argument. The disinclination to take seriously the study of the rhetorical organisation of texts gave rise to a surprisingly unhelpful tradition for the teaching of literature, which is with us yet in many places: 'civilising' it might be, but it was *not* to be the object of systematic study, for such study would in some ill-defined way threaten or devalue the work of literature itself.

A grammarian like Murray had never been in doubt about the relationship of grammar and rhetoric. As he examined it, grammar was concerned with the syntax of the written English sentence: it was not concerned with the study of 'style', about which he wrote a short appendix in his original grammar, where his debt to the major rhetoricians of the period was apparent. Rhetorical studies, especially as discussed by Campbell for instance, did address questions of 'style', always from the standpoint of a recognition of the close relationship of language to the socially created purpose in using language. In fact, the general model of language as discussed by Campbell bore some relationship to the model taken up in this series, most notably in its commitment to register.

The notion of register proposes a very intimate relationship of text to context: indeed, so intimate is that relationship, it is asserted, that the one can only be interpreted by reference to the other. Meaning is realised in language (in the form of text), which is thus shaped or patterned in response to the context of situation in which it is used. To study language then, is to concentrate upon exploring how it is systematically patterned towards important social ends. The linguistic theory adopted here is that of systemic linguistics. Such a linguistic theory is itself also a social theory, for it proposes firstly, that it is in the nature of human behaviour to build reality and/or experience through complex semiotic processes, and secondly, that the principal semiotic system available to humans is their language. In this sense, to study language is to explore some of the most important and pervasive of the processes by which human beings build their world.

I originally developed the volumes in this series as the basis of two major off campus courses in Language Education taught in the Master's degree program at Deakin University, Victoria, Australia. To the best of my knowledge, such courses, which are designed primarily for teachers and teacher educators, are the first of their kind in the world, and while they actually appeared in the mid 1980s, they emerge from work in language education which has been going on in Australia for some time. This included the national Language Development Project, to which Michael Halliday was consultant, and whose work I co-ordinated throughout its second, productive phase. (This major project was initiated by the Commonwealth Government's Curriculum Development Centre, Canberra, in the 1970s, and involved the co-operation of curriculum development teams from all Australian states in developing language curriculum materials. Its work was not completed because of political changes which caused the activities of the Curriculum Development Centre to be wound down.) In the 1980s a number of conferences have been held fairly regularly in different parts of Australia, all of them variously exploring aspects of language education, and leading to the publication of a number of conference reports. They include: Frances Christie (ed.), *Language and the Social Construction of Experience* (Deakin University, 1983); Brendan Bartlett and John Carr (eds.), *Language in Education Workshop: a Report of Proceedings* (Centre for Research and Learning, Brisbane C.A.E., Mount Gravatt Campus, Brisbane, 1984); Ruqaiya Hasan (ed.), *Discourse on Discourse* (Applied Linguistics Association of Australia, Occasional Papers, Number 7, 1985); Clare Painter and J.R. Martin (eds.), *Writing to Mean: Teaching Genres across the Curriculum* (Applied Linguistics Association of Australia, Occasional Papers, Number 9, 1986); Linda Gerot, Jane Oldenburg and Theo Van Leeuwen (eds.), *Language and Socialisation: Home and School* (in preparation). All these activities have contributed to the building of a climate of opinion and a tradition of thinking about language which made possible the development of the volumes in this series.

While it is true that the developing tradition of language education which these volumes represent does, as I have noted, take up some of the concerns of the older rhetorical studies, it nonetheless also looks forward, pointing to ways of examining language which were not available in earlier times. For example, the notion of language as a social semiotic, and its associated conception of experience or reality as socially built and constantly subject to processes of transformation, finds very much better expression today than would have been possible before, though obviously much more requires to be said about this than can be dealt with in these volumes. In addition, a functionally driven view of language is now available, currently most completely articulated in Halliday's *An Introduction to Functional Grammar* (1985), which offers ways of understanding the English language in a manner that Murray's Grammar could not have done.

Murray's Grammar confined itself to considerations of the syntax of the written English sentence. It did not have anything of use to say about spoken language, as opposed to written language, and, equally, it provided no basis upon which to explore a unit other than the sentence, whether that be the paragraph, or, even more importantly, the total text. The preoccupation with the written sentence reflected the pre-eminent position being accorded to the written word by Murray's time, leading to disastrous consequences since, that is the diminished value accorded to spoken language, especially in educational practices. In Murray's work, the lack of a direct relationship between the study of grammar on the one hand, and that of 'style', on the other hand, was, as I have already noted, to be attributed to his view that it was the rhetorician who addressed wider questions relating to the text. In the tradition in which he worked, in fact, grammar looked at syntactic rules divorced from considerations of meaning or social purpose.

By contrast, Halliday's approach to grammar has a number of real strengths, the first of which is the fact that its basis is semantic, not syntactic: that is to say, it is a semantically driven grammar, which, while not denying that certain principles of syntax do apply, seeks to consider and identify the role of various linguistic items in any text in terms of their function in building meaning. It is for this reason that its practices for interpreting and labelling various linguistic items and groupings are functionally based, not syntactically based. There is in other words, no dissociation of 'grammar' on the one hand and 'semantics' or meaning on the other. A second strength of Halliday's approach is that it is not uniquely interested in written language, being instead committed to the study of both the spoken and written modes, and to an explanation of the differences between the two, in such a way that each is illuminated because of its contrast with the other. A third and final strength of the systemic functional grammar is that it permits useful movement across the text, addressing the manner in which linguistic patternings are built up for the construction of the overall text in its particular 'genre', shaped as it is in response to the context of situation which gave rise to it.

Halliday's functional grammar lies behind all ten volumes in this series, though one other volume, by Michael Christie, called *Aboriginal perspectives on experience and learning: the role of language in Aboriginal Education*, draws upon somewhat different if still compatible perspectives in educational and language theory to develop its arguments. The latter volume, is available directly from Deakin University. In varying ways, the volumes in this series provide a helpful introduction to much that is more fully dealt with in Halliday's Grammar, and I commend the series to the reader who wants to develop some sense of the ways such a body of linguistic theory can be applied to educational questions. A version of the grammar specifically designed for teacher education remains to be written, and while I cherish ambitions to begin work on such a version soon, I am aware that others have similar ambitions — in itself a most desirable development.

While I have just suggested that the reader who picks up any of the volumes in this series should find ways to apply systemic linguistic theory to educational theory, I want to argue, however, that what is offered here is more than merely a course in applied linguistics, legitimate though such a course might be. Rather, I want to claim that this is a course in educational linguistics, a term of importance because it places linguistic study firmly at the heart of educational enquiry. While it is true that a great deal of linguistic research of the past, where it did not interpret language in terms of interactive, social processes, or where it was not grounded in a concern for meaning, has had little of relevance to offer education, socially relevant traditions of linguistics like that from which systemics is derived, do have a lot to contribute. How that contribution should be articulated is quite properly a matter of development in partnership between educationists, teachers and linguistics, and a great deal has yet to be done to achieve such articulation.

I believe that work in Australia currently is making a major contribution to the development of a vigorous educational linguistics, not all of it of course in a systemic framework. I would note here the important work of such people as J.R. Martin, Joan Rothery, Suzanne Eggins and Peter Wignell of the University of Sydney, investigating children's writing development; the innovatory work of Brian Gray and his colleagues a few years ago in developing language programs for Aboriginal children in central Australia, and more recently his work with other groups in Canberra; the recent work of Beth Graham, Michael Christie and Stephen Harris, all of the Northern Territory Department of Education, in developing language programs for Aboriginal children; the important work of John Carr and his colleagues of the Queensland Department of Education in developing new perspectives upon language in the various language curriculum guidelines they have prepared for their state; the contributions of Jenny Hammond of the University of Wollongong, New South Wales, in her research into language development in schools, as well as the various programs in which she teaches; research being undertaken by Ruqaiya Hasan and Carmel Cloran of Macquarie University, Sydney, into children's language learning styles in the transition years from home to school; investigations by Linda Gerot, also of Macquarie University, into classroom discourse in the secondary school, across a number of different subjects; and the work of Pam Gilbert of James Cook University, Townsville, in Queensland, whose interests are both in writing in the secondary school, and in language and gender.

The signs are that a coherent educational linguistics is beginning to appear around the world, and I note with pleasure the appearance of two new and valuable international journals: *Language and Education*, edited by David Corson of Massey University, New Zealand, and *Linguistics in Education*, edited by David Bloome, of the University of Massachusetts. Both are committed to the development of an educational linguistics, to which many traditions of study, linguistic, semiotic and sociological, will no doubt make an important contribution. Such an educational linguistics is long overdue, and in what are politically difficult times, I suggest such a study can make a major contribution to the pursuit of educational equality of opportunity, and to attacking the wider social problems of equity and justice. Language is a political institution: those who are wise in its ways, capable of using it to shape and serve important personal and social goals, will be the ones who are 'empowered' (to use a fashionable word): able, that is, not merely to participate effectively *in* the world, but able also *to act upon it*, in the sense that they can strive for significant social change. Looked at in these terms, provision of appropriate language education programs is a profoundly important matter, both in ensuring equality of educational opportunity, and in helping to develop those who are able and willing to take an effective role in democratic processes of all kinds.

One of the most encouraging measures of the potential value of the perspectives open to teachers taking up an educational linguistics of the kind offered in these monographs, has been the variety of teachers attracted to the courses of which they form a part, and the ways in which these teachers have used what they have learned in undertaking research papers for the award of the master's degree. They include, for example, secondary teachers of physics, social science, geography and English, specialists in teaching English as a second language to migrants and specialists in teaching English to Aboriginal people, primary school teachers, a nurse educator, teachers of illiterate adults, and language curriculum consultants, as well as a number of teacher educators with specialist responsibilities in teaching language education. For many of these people the perspectives offered by an educational linguistics are both new and challenging, causing them to review and change aspects of their teaching practices in various ways. Coming to terms with a semantically driven grammar is in itself quite demanding, while there is often considerable effort involved to bring to conscious awareness the ways in which we use language for the realisation of different meanings. But the effort is plainly worth it, principally because of the added sense of control and direction it can give teachers interested to work at fostering and developing students who are independent and confident in using language for the achievement of various goals. Those people for whom these books have proved helpful, tend to say that they have achieved a stronger and richer appreciation of language and how it works than they had before; that because they know considerably more about language themselves, they are able to intervene much more effectively in directing and guiding those whom they teach; that because they have a better sense of the relationship of language and 'content' than they had before, they can better guide their students into control of the 'content' of the various subjects for which they are responsible; and finally, that because they have an improved sense of how to direct language learning, they are able to institute new assessment policies, negotiating, defining and clarifying realistic goals for their students. By any standards, these are considerable achievements.

As I draw this Foreword to a close, I should perhaps note for the reader's benefit the manner in which students doing course work with me are asked to read the monographs in this series, though I should stress that the books were deliberately designed to be picked up and read in any order one likes. In the first of the two semester courses, called *Language and Learning*, students are asked to read the following volumes in the order given:

Frances Christie — *Language education*
Clare Painter — *Learning the mother tongue*
M.A.K. Halliday & Ruqaiya Hasan — *Language, context, and text: aspects of language in a social-semiotic perspective*
J.L. Lemke — *Using language in the classroom*
then either,
M.A.K. Halliday — *Spoken and written language*
or,
Ruqaiya Hasan — *Linguistics, language, and verbal art.*

The following four volumes, together with the one by Michael Christie, mentioned above, belong to the second course called *Sociocultural Aspects of Language and Education*, and they may be read by the students in any order they like, though only three of the five need be selected for close study:

David Butt — *Talking and thinking: the patterns of behaviour*
Gunther Kress — *Linguistic processes in sociocultural practice*
J.R. Martin — *Factual writing: exploring and challenging social reality*
Cate Poynton — *Language and gender: making the difference*

References

Bain, A., *An English Grammar* (Longman, Roberts and Green, London, 1863).

Bain, A., *English Composition and Rhetoric*, revised in two Parts — *Part 1, Intellectual Elements of Style*, and *Part 11, Emotional Qualities of Style* (Longman, Green and Company, London, 1887).

Ballard, P., *Teaching the Mother Tongue* (Hodder & Stoughton, London, 1921).

Blair, H., *Lectures on Rhetoric and Belles Lettres, Vols. 1 and 11* (W. Strahan and T. Cadell, London, 1783).

Campbell, G., (new ed.), *The Philosophy of Rhetoric* (T. Tegg and Son, London, 1838). Originally published (1776).

Halliday, M.A.K., *Language as social semiotic: the social interpretation of language and meaning* (Edward Arnold, London, 1978).

Halliday, M.A.K., *An Introduction to Functional Grammar* (Edward Arnold, London, 1985).

Murray, Lindley, *English Grammar* (1795), Facsimile Reprint No. 106 (Menston, Scolar Press, 1968).

Contents

Factual writing: exploring and challenging social reality

Chapter 1

Stories and facts

Recounts

Text 1.1
Q: Do you remember how you first got into breeding?
A: Yeah, quite by accident [laughter].
Q: Can you tell me?
A: Yeah . . . A friend, she got a little puppy, and I just fell in love with it. And then they told me that there was still one left in the litter, so I went and bought her. No way in the world I'd even thought about showing or breeding or anything like that. I'd always just liked dogs. So, we bought this one and she was terrible. In fact, I think she's the worst dog I've ever seen. Except, she had a terrific nature and there's no way in the world I'd ever get rid of her. Still got her. And . . . we just went from there. We bought another one, and . . . another one, and . . . eventually we've got eight. [laughter]

People tell stories—during meals, at the pub, in coffee shops, and even in more formal situations such as the interview conducted by Guenter Plum underlying Text 1.1. These stories are about what has happened, usually to the person telling the story. In casual conversation we mostly talk about ourselves—what we did, how we feel, and what we think. Life is rushing by—event after event, day after day. We are caught up in it. Only our memories and the stories we pull out of them keep life from disappearing almost as it happens. We use language to keep the past alive.

People who speak languages with writing systems have more than their memories to go on. They can, if they wish, make permanent records of what has happened. Many people use a diary in this way to keep track of things. And young children, very soon after first learning to write, use language in this way. They write about what has happened to them: playing with friends, visits to relatives, trips and so on. Text 1.2 is from a Year 2 student in Liverpool, Sydney, writing about what happened on a school excursion. This type of story will be referred to as a RECOUNT.

Text 1.2   Our excursion

We went to an Excursion. The man took us there and on the way we got caught in a traffic jam and waited. Then we were in Sydney and the bus stopped and everyone got out. We went into the museum and we put our bags in the cupboard. Then we went to see a film called 'A Message from a Dinosaur'. Then we had lunch and I had some fruit. Then we went back to school. (Year 2)

In many respects this young child's written story resembles the story spoken by the adult in Text 1.1. Both texts are about something that the narrator has personally experienced. The stories are built up around a sequence of actions: getting into dog breeding and going on a school excursion. The events which form the backbone of each text are listed in Figure 1.1.

Figure 1.1   The sequence of events in Texts 1.1 and 1.2

getting into dog breeding

1. friend buys dog
2. narrator falls in love with it
3. narrator learns of other dog
4. narrator goes and buys it
5. narrator buys another dog
6. narrator ends up with eight dogs

going to the museum

1. writer gets caught in traffic jam
2. writer arrives in Sydney
3. the bus stops
4. everyone gets out
5. class enters museum
6. class puts bags in cupboard
7. class sees film
8. class eats lunch
9. writer has some fruit
10. class returns to school

There are, of course, differences between the two texts. The major difference has to do with the expression of feelings in Text 1.1: *I just fell in love with it*, *I'd always just liked dogs*, *she was terrible*, *she's the worst dog I've ever seen*, and so on. At no stage in Text 1.2, on the other hand, does the child tell us how she felt about the trip. In this respect Texts 1.1 and 1.2 illustrate one of the major differences between speech and writing in our culture. In general, speech is personal—we say what we feel; and, in general, writing is impersonal— we write about what has happened or what we think, but not usually about how we feel. It would be wrong to say that something is missing in Text 1.2. Quite the contrary. We should give the young writer credit for recognising at a very early stage that writing is impersonal. This is an important lesson to learn when children are figuring out how to write effectively.

The impersonality of writing bothers some people. They find it cold and alienating. Especially in the case of young children learning to write, some people quite sincerely worry about this apparently repressive aspect of writing and try to encourage children to write more expressively. This kind of attitude is one factor which leads to the emergence of the story as the most frequent kind of writing attempted by children in infants' and primary school in Australia. Stories do allow more scope,

4

through dialogue and character development, for children to use express-ive language. And this aspect of narrative is likely to be one of the reasons why stories are so highly valued in our culture.

The development of narrative writing in young children and the function of mature narrative in our culture is a fascinating and worth-while inquiry, but not something that we will be pursuing here. Instead, in this book, we will move off in a different direction, and look at writing which is not about what happened, but which is about the way things are. I will refer to writing about the way things are as **factual** writing, of which there are several kinds. We will begin with a kind of factual writing which resembles the Recounts we have just con-sidered in some respects but differs along one crucial dimension.

Procedure writing

Probably the closest type of factual writing to narrative is PROCEDURE writing. This is because, like narrative, procedural texts are built up around a sequence of events. Text 1.3 is an example of this kind of writing from a student in Year 3.

Text 1.3
If you want to grow beans the first thing you do is go to a shop and get a packet of bean seeds. buy them. bring Them home. plant them in the garden water every foow days water them. When they grow your pick them. send them to the froot macker. and then someone buys them. they take them home and eat them. (Year 3)

One very useful exercise when working on different genres is to rewrite texts from one genre into another, keeping as much of the actual content as possible the same. Procedural texts are similar enough to Recounts that this is quite easy. Young writers may in fact shift back and forth between the two genres without realising it. Told as a Recount, Text 1.3 would come out as Text 1.4.

Text 1.4
We wanted to grow beans, so we went to the shop and bought a packet of bean seeds. Then we brought them home and planted them in the garden. We watered them every few days and when they grew we picked them. Then we sent them to the fruit market. Someone bought them and took them home and ate them.

What is the difference between Texts 1.3 and 1.4? The crucial difference might be characterised in terms of generality. Text 1.3 is about how to grow beans, and talks generally about how to do this. The people, places, and things in Text 1.3 are all general: *you* refers to people in general, not to the reader; similarly *beans* refers to beans as a class. The actions in Text 1.3 are also general; so the verbs are timeless, referring not to what someone did, or is doing, or will do, but to what they do in general. The young writer achieves this in two ways. Sometimes she uses the simple present tense: *the first thing you do*, *someone buys them*; alternatively, she uses imperative clauses which are not marked for tense at all: *buy them*, *bring Them home*. Procedural writing makes use of both possibilities, although in mature texts one alternative is selected and used consistently throughout.

The generality of both participants and events in procedural writing contrasts sharply with their specificity in Recounts. In Text 1.4, specific participants predominate. The *we* refers to particular people including the writer, and *a packet of bean seeds* refers to a specific collection of bean seeds. And the events are specific as well—things that actually happened. Thus the use of past tense forms: *we went to the shop*, *we brought them home*. In other words Recounts are about something that actually happened (including the products of people's imaginations). Procedural texts, on the other hand, are about how things happen.

Procedural writing, because it is so close to Recount writing, is a natural place to begin when encouraging children to move from narrative to factual genres. Of course care must be taken that Recounts and Procedures are not confused. And different types of procedural writing need to be noted. One type of procedural writing, what we might call INSTRUCTIONS, consists of a sequence of imperative clauses (as in a recipe): *In order to grow beans, go to the shop, get a packet of bean seeds and buy them. Then bring them home*. Another, which we might call DIRECTIONS, uses declarative clauses in the simple present tense with a generalised Actor realised by *you* (and less frequently *we* or *one*): *In order to grow beans, you go to the shop, you get a packet of bean seeds and you buy them. Then you bring them home*. Again, care must be taken that when children select either Instructions or Directions that they write consistently that genre. Text 1.3 is really a mixture of the two.

Depending on their age (and there is no reason why this could not begin in infants' school), children's attention should be drawn to the main differences between Recounts and Procedures. Procedures are general, about how things are done. They describe the way the world is, focusing on events. In this sense Procedures can be seen to explore the world in a way that Recounts do not. Recounts are examples of how things get done; they do not generalise beyond particular experiences. All narrative writing is in fact limited in this way. This is why we have developed factual genres in our culture—to go beyond particular experience, in order to interpret and understand. Children do, of course, learn through narrative, as through all their experience of language. But the learning involved in factual writing is of a different kind.

Young children can be encouraged from an early age to recognise differences between genres.

Report writing

So far we have been concentrating on events, and the way in which sequences of events contribute to the structure of Recounts and Procedures. But what about things? What if we take people, places, and things rather than what they do as the focus of our writing? Take relatives, for example, as in Text 1.5.

6

Text 1.5   Where did my family come from
My dad came from England.
My Mum came from Australia.
My Nana came from Australia.
My popa come from Australia.
My great grandmother came from Australia.
My great grandfather come from Scotland.
My great, great granmother came from Ireland.
I don't no any more so good bye. (Year 3)

The purpose of Text 1.5 is very different from that of Texts 1.1—4. Instead of telling what happens, it describes. The writer focuses on her relatives and describes where they come from. We can refer to texts which focus on particular individuals and specify some of their characteristics as DESCRIPTIONS.

A closely related genre to Descriptions, which focuses on classes of things rather than individuals, is the REPORT. Note that in Text 1.6, a Report, it is birds in general that are characterised; the writer does not have any particular bird in mind.

Text 1.6   Birds
Birds live up in a tree. If they don't eat they die.
Redbirds balckbirds any colored birds Dark birds light birds. Some are small and others are big. (Year 3)

You may have noticed that the difference between Descriptions and Reports is very similar to that between Recounts and Procedures. Like Procedures, Reports make general, not specific, statements. If we try and change Text 1.6 into a Description we would get something like Text 1.7.

Procedures and Reports generalise experience.

Text 1.7   Birds
My bird lived up in a tree. It ate so it wouldn't die. It was a black bird and it was small.

We could, of course, have done the same thing in the other direction, changing Text 1.5 into a Report, producing a text like Text 1.8.

Text 1.8   Australian immigration
Australians come from many different countries, including England, Ireland and Scotland. Many Australians were born right here in Australia.

So Descriptions are, in fact, examples of Reports, just as Recounts are examples of Procedures. Both Procedures and Reports then generalise particular experiences. As was suggested with Recounts and Procedures earlier, by focusing children's attention on the fundamental differences between Descriptions and Reports, teachers could help children learn to write consistently in each genre. The relationship between the four genres considered to this point is summed up in Figure 1.2.

Is it possible to mix Descriptions with Reports by having specific participants and general events? Try writng a text of this type.

7

Figure 1.2 Recounts, Procedures, Descriptions, and Reports—how they are alike and different in terms of generality and focus

	particular	general
event focus	Recount	Procedure
thing focus	Description	Report

Creativity and imagination in factual writing

Earlier we noted that some people are disturbed by the impersonal nature of writing in general and try to encourage narrative and poetic writing to overcome this. With factual writing (Procedures, Descriptions, and Reports) there is a related concern that little opportunity is provided in these genres for creativity and imagination. In fact, there is little cause for concern. Provided a child has mastered a genre, there will always be room for verbal play. In Text 1.9, for example, a Year 3 writer personifies himself as the wind and develops an 'imaginative' Report through this technique.

Text 1.9 I am the wind
I am the wind and I can blow tents down and I can blow a trees down and I can blow sheds down. (Year 3)

In Text 1.10, a Year 6 writer sends up the Procedure genre with her highly creative 'How to catch a fish'.

Text 1.10 How to catch a fish
You put on your oldest dirtiest clothes and bring with you a friend who knows how to fish. Get your friend to help you bait your hook then let him or her cast your line try to sit patiently. If you can't your friend could come in handy to talk with. [?] play some kind of game you can do sitting down. This is so you do not have to leave your spot. When you get a nibble close your eyes while you let your friend reel it in. Get your friend to show off his or her catch and take a photo. STAND CLEAR while your friend cleans, scales and guts the fish because the fish is going to smell. If you can't find a spot where the smell doesn't reach you it won't hurt to bring a peg. (Year 6)

From examples such as these we can see that factual writing need not stand in the way of creativity or imagination. Skilful writers are just as creative when writing in these genres as they are in their narrative texts. It is, however, necessary to introduce a word of caution here.

Factual and narrative writing serve different functions.

Factual writing and narratives are different, and they are different because they serve different functions in our culture. The main function of stories in our culture is to entertain, notwithstanding the small group of literary critics who take narrative very seriously indeed. This is not true of all cultures—in Aboriginal cultures, for example, myths and legends function as much to explain as to entertain. Arising out of this, stories positively encourage creativity and imagination. In fact, narrat-

8

ive is often taken as the model of what people mean by creative and imaginative writing (a rather misleading view of creativity and imagination as we have just seen).

Factual writing, on the other hand, has a different function. Factual writing is designed not to amuse us, but to explore the world around us. It focuses on how things get done and what things are like. So successful factual writing is about the world; it is not primarily intended to entertain.

In education it is important to appreciate the different functions of factual writing and narrative and to understand that the qualities that make for an effective Report will not be the same as those which lead to an entertaining narrative. Reports should not be judged on the basis of how creative or imaginative they are, any more than narratives should be judged on the basis of how much we learn from them. This is not to say that Reports can't be amusing, nor that narratives can't teach. It is simply to point out that the primary functions of these genres in our culture are different, and that these differences must be respected in any assessment procedure. Whenever criteria appropriate for evaluating one genre are applied to another, considerable confusion is certain to arise. One of the major problems children face at present in learning factual genres in infants' and primary school is that assessment criteria, both implicit and explicit, focus almost exclusively on narrative rather than on factual texts.

Developing Report writing

Having considered the place of creativity and imagination in factual writing, let us now return to the Report genre, beginning with another example of a Report, Text 1.11.

Text 1.11 Brachiosaurus
Brachiosaurus, the largest dinosaur of all, was three times as heavy as Apatosaurus. One skeleton has been found that is 30 metres long. When it was alive, this animal must have weighed more than fifteen times as much as a modern elephant. Brachiosaurus was a plant-eater. (Year 2)

As with Text 1.6 above, Text 1.11 focuses on classes of things and makes a number of general statements about them. However, unlike Text 1.6, Text 1.11 has one statement which is not general, but specific: *One skeleton has been found which is 30 metres long*. Taken out of context this is the kind of statement we would expect in a specific Recount or Description text rather than a generalising Report. What is it doing there?

How influential do you think the source of Text 1.11 has been? What could have been the source?

In fact, specific statements do have a place in Report writing in that they can be used to illustrate or exemplify a general point which is made. In Text 1.11, the statement that a 30 metre long skeleton has been found illustrates the preceding general statement that Brachiosaurus was the largest dinosaur of all. In a sense it is a piece of evidence, supporting the writer's more general claim. The use of specific statements to back up general ones is an important feature in the development of Report writing into Exposition. It is important to note that very young children are already capable of taking this step.

Yet another of the concerns shared by many teachers when it comes to Report writing is the question of originality. Like adults, children often depend on books, magazines, encyclopaedias, and so on for the information used in factual writing, and these resources do influence the texts which children then produce. Again it needs to be stressed that the genre itself does not prevent a child from drawing on her own experience in Report writing. Text 1.12, for example, is not derived from written sources, but represents an original piece of research by the writer.

The issue of originality in writing: children, like adults, must often draw on other sources as they write.

Text 1.12   Radios

Radios have been around for years. They come in all sizes. Tape recorders have six buttons. That's one for eject, one for stopping, one for starting, one for rewinding, one for forward and one for recording. There are three switches. One is for stereo and mono (mode), one is for tape, fm and am (function) and off and on (monitor). It also has a dial that puts it on different stations. The stations are 2WS, 2SM, 2JJJ, 2UW, 2EA, 3EA, 2UE, M.M.M. and 2GB. On tape recorders there are two wide speakers. Also there are two volume dials. It has from zero (min) to ten (max). Our tape recorder is a P.Y.E. sre4032. There is a place where you can attach you ear phones to. In the back there is a little place where you can put the batteries in. (Year 3)

At the same time it needs to be pointed out that Reports function in our culture to store information. Children, like adults, have access to far more information through reading than they do through their own experience, and it is natural for them to draw on this in Report writing. Once again it is important to stress that the standards of originality which apply to narrative writing cannot be applied to writing whose function is radically different. Learning to access information which is stored in books and other written forms is an important skill which needs to be encouraged in the development of any young writer.

Like Text 1.11, Text 1.12 also makes use of specific statements: e.g. *Our tape recorder is a P.Y.E. sre4032.* These statements do not appear to be functioning as illustrations of any of the generalisations made earlier in the Report and we suspect that this writer is moving from Report to Description at this stage of his text. This kind of slippage may need to be drawn to the attention of young writers who frequently fail to write consistently within either the Description or Report genre.

Earlier in Text 1.12, on the other hand, the writer shifts effectively from the general to the more particular three times. He introduces the buttons, then describes the uses of each; then he mentions switches and their function; and finally dials and the stations available. This means that, unlike the Reports considered earlier, Text 1.12 is more than a random collection of facts. Its information is organised into sets. Organising information in this way is another important step towards the development of paragraphs and later the arrangement of arguments in expository writing. Headings may be used to highlight internal organisation of this kind as in Text 1.13, a Report from a more mature writer in Year 6.

What kind of headings might the writer have used in Text 1.12?

10

Text 1.13   Coelacanth—The living fossil!
Where it lives: The Coelacanth lives off the East Coast of South Arfica, between the mainland and the island of Malagasy. They live at depths ranging from 400 to 1500 feet.
How it protects itself: The Coelacanth protects itself because of its size and a think, black, greasy oil it exudes.
Special features: The Coelacanth has lobe-shaped fins and until 1938 it was thought to be extinct. In that year a fishing trawler caught one off the South African Coast.
Does it have any use to man, e.g., food: The Coelacanth is used for nothing except food and is eaten very rarely. The Coelacanth ranges from Blue to Muddy Brown. (Year 6)

Explanations

So far we have looked at three basic types of factual writing: Procedures, Descriptions, and Reports. Procedures are about how things get done. Descriptions and Reports are about what things are like. You may have noticed as we worked through our examples of the genres that these three genres do not really try to explain anything. The texts say how and what, but don't really answer the question why. For this reason causal relations are rare in Procedures, Descriptions, and Reports.

Some Reports do contain explanations. In Text 1.14, for example, a reason is given for the hard shell snails carry around with them.

Text 1.14
Snails have a shell on their back <u>to protect them selfs from enemy</u>.they like to hide behind a rock and it leavs a silvery track behide him. A snail has a strong foot. They stick to the ground fermilee. (Year 2)

But the function of the Report genre as a whole is to describe in general terms, not explain; so explanations form, at best, just a part of the meaning of the text overall.

In our research into the development of children's writing in Sydney we have found very little in the way of explanatory texts in infants' and primary school. EXPLANATIONS are so rare that we need to be cautious about setting them up as a genre at this stage. However, Text 1.15 is an example of writing of this kind from Year 3.

See Martin & Rothery (1980, 1981, 1986) and Martin (1984).

Text 1.15
A friend is important to me because if you don't have a friend you never play. (Year 3)

There are two important things to note about this text. Firstly, like Procedures and Reports, it is general—it explains why friends are important, not why the writer likes one particular friend. Secondly, note that this Explanation focuses on a judgment made by the writer—that friends are important. Judgments involve the writer interpreting the world, not simply observing it. Saying that something is important means adopting an attitude towards it. Justifying attitudes seems to be the most common use of Explanations in the writing of young children.

In a sense this is highly significant. It seems that children have learned something important about one of the main differences between speech and writing—that writing is impersonal. In general, writing discourages the overt expression of feelings and attitudes. And when they are expressed they must be explicitly justified. Teachers may need to spend time with certain children pointing out the places in their factual writing where judgments are made and encouraging an Explanation in these contexts. The way in which the teacher has formed her question in Text 1.16 has likely been helpful in focusing children's attention on this point.

Text 1.16 Who were the Vikings? Why were they famous?
The Vikings were Scandinavian and the first world explorers. The Vikings were famous for their exploration voyages and their fighting ability. (Year 6)

An example of a more developed explanatory text is given in Text 1.17. Note again the judgement involved in selecting **favourite** things and the subsequent justification of each choice.

Text 1.17 Things I would miss!
If I had to give up my five favourite things they would be my: TV set, Bed, Clothes, House Food. I would miss my TV because I would miss my favourite programs. I would miss my bed because I would have no where comfortable to sleep. I would miss my clothes because I would be cold. I would miss my House because I would have no where dry to go. I would miss food because I would starve. (Year 6)

It seems that explanatory writing is very rare in infants' and primary schools.

As noted above, explanatory writing is very rare at present in infants' and primary school in NSW. At one school we examined, it amounted to only about a half of 1 per cent of the writing done. This means that children are not gaining experience in developing the argumentation needed in expository texts.

Sexism and factual writing

Before turning to Exposition proper, some comments need to be made about the differences between boys and girls as far as factual writing is concerned. Firstly, unless the teacher sets up specific tasks as part of a thematic unit, boys and girls will tend to write about different things. Most readers will have no trouble in assigning the Report in Text 1.18 to a female writer, especially when comparing it with Text 1.13 above, which was written by a boy in the same class.

Text 1.18 Gold fish
Gold fish are rather nice as they swim around in their pond. Their name is Gold but it is not always so as they are quite orange. They swim around hunting for food. They are always hungry. Some like to hide under a rock or in between some reeds, but some show-off and then swim off and they are never seen again. (Year 6)

One way of seeing this difference between boys and girls as far as factual writing is concerned is to say that boys are interested in the **nature**, girls in the **nurture**, of things. This leads not only to a different choice of subject-matter in factual writing (as in narrative), but to the greater interest shown in factual writing by boys. We have noted in our work that when given a free choice of topic and genre, boys choose to write Reports much more frequently than girls; although girls write Reports perfectly well when teachers ask them to do so. This preference puts boys at something of a disadvantage in writing contexts where creativity, originality, and imagination are being emphasised. A boy's effective Report will not normally be ranked with a girl's skilful narrative in terms of these qualities. Because of the latent preference for narrative writing in many teachers' expectations, boys' interest in factual writing actually puts them at a disadvantage in primary school. They will, of course, more than make up for this in secondary school when success or failure will come to depend far more on Exposition than on narrative. Nevertheless, it should be noted that a kind of 'inverse sexism' is practised in many Australian infants' and primary schools which encourages and rewards girls' interest in non-factual writing and is partly responsible for the different preferences boys and girls express for science, social science, English, and languages in the secondary curriculum.

Exposition

Ironically, in light of the sex differences just noted, the only piece of expository writing we managed to collect in 1983 from the infants' and primary school in which we were working was done by a girl in Year 6. This perhaps serves as a warning that the differences we noted above are social tendencies, not rules!

What is EXPOSITION proper? How does it differ from Reports and Explanations? In a sense, Expositions are simply more fully developed Explanations. The main difference is that in Exposition the judgment which needs to be explained is one which is treated as more socially significant and which therefore takes longer to justify. To begin, let's briefly review the judgments in Texts 1.15, 1.16, and 1.17:

1.15. A friend is important to me . . .

1.16. The Vikings were famous . . .

1.17. I would miss my favourite things (i.e. TV, Bed, clothes, House, Food) . . .

Note that five distinct judgments are included in Text 1.17, one for each of the favorite things, and that justification is given for each of these.

Once we have isolated these judgments from the rest of their text, it is possible to imagine Expositions rather than Explanations having been built up around them. This would have involved far more than a simple justification for each. In Text 1.19, for example, from the same writing context as Text 1.16, the writer is on her way to developing an expository text in this way.

Text 1.19 Who were the Phonecians? Why are they famous?
The Phonecians were one of the great peoples of the ancient world. They were great sailors, navigators and traders. They became famous in history for two achievements. They were among the first to send out explorers and colonies throughout the Mediterranean Sea area, and even beyond the Strait of Gibraltar. (Year 6)

Significantly, the writer alerts the reader to the fact that two arguments are going to be presented as justification for the judgment that the Phonecians were famous: *They became famous in history for two achievements*. Here the writer employs the very useful expository technique of naming her arguments (*two achievements*), relating them causally to her judgment with a preposition (*for*), and then going on to list the two arguments in favour of the thesis. Unfortunately this does not quite come off as it is not clear from what follows which argument is which. In mature Exposition this would have to be clearly specified, often with conjunctions such as *first . . . second*.

Note the distinction between Explanation and Exposition.

It looks then as if we might be able to distinguish between Explanation and Exposition along the following lines. In Exposition, more than one argument is presented in favour of a judgment. We will refer to the judgment in Exposition as a THESIS, and to the reasons supporting it as ARGUMENTS. In mature Exposition each Argument for the Thesis tends to form a paragraph, and the Arguments and Thesis may be summed up in a final paragraph or CONCLUSION. These features evolve over time in children's writing. In Text 1.20, for example, several arguments are presented in favour of the Thesis that the best pet in the world is a pet rock. But the Arguments are simply listed rather than being organised into paragraphs which focus on and develop each point. A mature writer might have selected just some of these arguments to make her case.

Text 1.20 The perfect pet
The best pet in the world is a pet that you don't have to feed, doesn't fidget and doesn't make noises in the middle of the night. The pet that fits all these categories is a pet rock! you never have to worry about it dying because it was never alive in the first place. When you take your pet rock for a walk you don't have to worry about it fighting with another rock. You don't ever have to wash it or brush its fur. Pet rocks are also good for weather predictions. If your rock is wet you know its raining, when it starts to fly its windy and when it shakes it must be an earthquake. A pet rock will never run away, it doesn't answer back and if you don't like the colour of the rock you can paint it again. The food bill is very low for a pet rock for it will cost you nothing to feed. There are two or three things your pet rock will not do. It will not fetch a ball or stick, won't beg for food, and can't roll over for you to rub its stomach. But it also never digs up the garden and doesn't care if you change its name. Pet rocks never catch a cold or get sunburnt. They are very good for paper weights if they are heavy. Last, but not least they can be both an indoor and outdoor pet. (Year 6)

Text 1.20 is not devoid of the organising principles that marshall arguments in mature Exposition. The writer's final argument is

14

introduced as such: *Last, but not least*. And in *There are two or three things your pet rock will not do* the writer uses a technique similar to that she exploited less successfully in Text 1.19 above: she uses a nominal expression, *two or three things*, to warn the reader that she is about to make some points about what pet rocks won't do, and then goes on to list these. Young writers such as this are clearly on their way to formulating mature Exposition. The resources needed for organising arguments in support of a thesis are already present. All that is needed is a little explicit guidance from the teacher about how to deploy them more effectively. Unfortunately, this kind of assistance is not usually provided for students by infants' and primary teachers in current practice.

Before summing up this first part of the book, we need to hark back to the section 'Creativity and imagination in factual writing' and emphasise once again that factual writing does not preclude creativity and imagination, as many teachers fear. Text 1.20 is a humorous and entertaining text by any standards, while at the same time fulfilling the generic requirements of the Exposition genre. So while Expositions do not normally function to entertain in our culture, they **can** serve this rhetorical purpose whenever a writer wishes to design them in this way. In essence, creativity has much more to do with mastering a genre and then adjusting it to meet one's own purposes than with writing stories 90 per cent of the time one puts pen to paper. It is surely creativity of this more general and practical kind that schools need to foster in young writers.

Creativity in writing involves mastering genres and adjusting them to suit one's own purposes.

Factual writing: summary

In this introductory chapter on factual writing we have seen that in spite of the preoccupation with narrative and expressive writing in Australian infants' and primary schools many children do develop factual genres of different kinds. The main types of factual writing uncovered were as follows:

Procedure	'how something is done'
Description	'what some particular thing is like'
Report	'what an entire class of things is like'
Explanation	'a reason why a judgment has been made'
Exposition	'arguments why a thesis has been proposed'

Only Reports occurred in large numbers in the infants' and primary school in which we have been working; from early in infants' school many children take an interest in writing of this kind. The lack of support given to this and other factual genres has very serious consequences when children arrive in secondary school and is indicative of a number of hidden attitudes and prejudices about children and writing held by many teachers. We will return to a sociocultural interpretation of these in Chapter 4. In Chapter 2, we will look at the functions of expository writing in our culture in more detail.

Chapter 2

Types of Exposition: 'persuading that' and 'persuading to'

Analytical and Hortatory Exposition

The focal element of an Exposition is its Thesis. One of the most effective ways of distinguishing different types of Exposition is to take this element, the Thesis, and look more closely at what is being argued for. In Text 1.20, for example, the Thesis was formulated as follows: *The best pet in the world is . . . a pet rock.* Let's now compare Text 1.20 with Text 2.1, a letter to the editor written by another Year 6 student.

Text 2.1

> 6 L. . .. Drive
> Mt Pritchard 2170
> 6.4.81

Dear Editor,
I am writing because of my concern over the fatalities caused through the misuse of firearms. I feel all governments should pass firmer laws on the control of firearms. Small firearms should only be issued under a license to responsible people such as policemen and security guards. Large firearms should only be owned and used by gunclubs and their members. This would cease the hunting and slaughter of our wildlife. Recent examples of firearm accidents are—Ronald Reagan's attempted assasination, an innocent eighteen year old shot by an angry boyfriend and a six year old boy killed while playing with a gun at a friends house. The Government are to afraid of losing their place because of the communities opinion of firearms. Life is to precious to be lost in this tragic way.

> Yours faithfully,
> . . ... (Year 6)

What about the Thesis in Text 2.1? Here we would need to formulate something along the lines of: *All governments should pass firmer laws on the control of firearms.* By comparing the two theses we can see that the function of Text 2.1 is quite different from that of Text 1.20. Both texts present a Thesis and argue for it. But in Text 2.1 an attempt is made to change the world. The Thesis is a COMMAND, not a STATEMENT. The writer is not simply analysing the world as it is and

16

defending this interpretation. Rather, she is challenging the world as she sees it, and making a suggestion as to how it should be changed. One way of looking at this difference is to say that the function of Text 1.20 is to persuade readers **that** the Thesis is well formulated, whereas in Text 2.1 the function of the text is to persuade the reader **to** do what the Thesis recommends.

The traditional name for Exposition that 'persuades **to**' is HORTA-TORY. Exposition which 'persuades **that**'has no special name in opposition to this; we will refer to it here simply as ANALYTICAL Exposition. Hortatory Exposition is commonly found in editorials, letters to the editor, sermons, political speeches and debates, office memos about employees' behaviour, and so on. Analytical Exposition is more typical of lectures, seminars, tutorials, scholarly papers, essay writing, and examination answers. In general, in our culture, Hortatory texts are either spoken, or if written, exhibit a number of the characteristics of spoken English. Analytical texts, on the other hand, tend to be written, and if spoken, to share many of the features of written language. In order to explore some of these differences let's look at Text 2.1, the Hortatory text, in more detail.

Hortatory Exposition 'persuades to', while Analytical Exposition 'persuades that'.

Hortatory Exposition

To begin, as a glance at Text 2.1 tells us, a number of the text's features have to do with the fact that it is a letter. The writer's address is given, the letter is addressed to the Editor, and signed by the writer. The fact that this Exposition is being channelled through the post is also responsible for the first sentence, which explains to the editor why the student is writing. The second sentence then introduces the Thesis of the text— the suggestion that governments pass firmer laws on gun control. We will not be following up the influence of mode (or channel) on texts here. It is important to note however that the term *letter* refers to a mode and not to a genre. We write letters for lots of different reasons: job applications, party invitations, thank-you notes, personal letters to friends, and so on. As a channel, letters can be used to transmit all kinds of different genres.

This distinction between the purpose of a text (genre) and the way in which it is transmitted (mode) is an important one because so many of our folk-linguistic terms confuse mode and genre. *Letters to the editor*, for example, are usually Hortatory Expositions sent through the mail and have much more in common with sermons and political speeches than with other types of letter. But the everyday term for the genre (i.e. *letter* to the editor) tends to obscure these similarities and differences.

The overall structure of Text 2.1 is basically as follows:

1. reason for writing
2. thesis (governments should pass firmer gun control laws)
3. examples of how gun control laws could be firmed up
4. first argument for thesis (protecting wildlife)
5. real examples of misuse of firearms (second argument for Thesis?)
6. reason why Governments are afraid to act
7. main reason why goverments should act anyhow.

17

Essentially two arguments are presented in favour of firmer gun control laws. One is that this would help protect wildlife. The other is that it would help end tragic firearm accidents. Clearly the Exposition could have been better organised to highlight these arguments. The presentation of the first argument is adequate: *This would cease the hunting and slaughter of our wildlife*; but the relation of the second argument to the Thesis is not really made explicit: *Recent examples of firearm accidents are . . ..* Examples are given of recent firearm accidents—but the effect of firmer gun control laws on the reduction of these is left implicit (until perhaps the final sentence of the text— *Life is to precious to be lost in this tragic way*). The examples of firearm accidents really need to be preceded by some statement to the effect that firmer laws would cut down on accidents as well as protecting wildlife. Constructive teaching could well have intervened at this point. As it is, the examples are too specific to directly support the Thesis. They needed to be generalised, and related causally to the writer's proposal.

This brings us to three important points which will be developed in the following sections, namely:

1. How **do** writers reason in Expository texts?;
2. How **personal** can Hortatory Expositions be?; and
3. How are **metaphors** used in Exposition?

Reasoning in Exposition

Expositions are about 'why'.

At the core of every form of Exposition is some form of reasoning. The function of Exposition is to interpret and explain, so realising cause and effect are important. Expositions are about **why**. For this reason we need to look at the ways in which languages like English express reasoning. These grammatical resources have to be deployed effectively if students are to write effective expository texts.

There are four main ways in which a language like English realises reasoning. Three of these are in fact illustrated in Text 2.1. Let's begin with the most straightforward. Consider the final sentence of Text 2.1:

Life is to precious to be lost in this tragic way.

This sentence in fact consists of two clauses: *Life is to precious* and *to be lost in this tragic way*. And there is a causal relation between the two, signalled by the purposive word *too* and the infinitive form of the verb in the second clause. This relation may be easier to see if we rewrite the sentence as follows:

Life is very precious; so it should not be lost in this tragic way.

Many languages would in fact have to express this meaning in the second version since not all languages have a word like *too*. In the revised version the causal conjunction *so* is used to explicitly signal the reasoning involved in connecting the two clauses. The first clause is now clearly marked as a reason, the second as a conclusion. Setting up two separate clauses, and marking the causal relation between them with a conjunction is the commonest way of reasoning in spoken language. In mature writing however, it is somewhat rare.

18

How else can languages do it? Consider now the first sentence in Text 2.1:

I am writing because of my concern over the fatalities caused through the misuse of firearms.

This time the reasoning is coded through the prepositional phrase *because of my concern*, not another clause (with *because of* as preposition and *my concern* as its complement). Compare this with the interclause method we just looked at:

I am writing because I am concerned about the . . .

As an exercise, you might try converting sentences back and forth in this way, and seeing what changes result.

When prepositional phrases are used to code reasoning, a preposition signals the causal relation instead of a conjunction; as well, what would have come out as a verb when two clauses are used is turned into a noun—*I am concerned* becomes *my concern*. We had another example of reasoning with prepositional phrases in Text 1.19 (i.e. *for two achievements*):

They became famous in history for two achievements.

Compare this with:

They became famous in history because they achieved two things.

Once again, what comes out as a verb when conjunctions are used comes out as a noun with prepositions.

Alongside using conjunctions and prepositions to express reasoning, English also makes use of verbs. There is a good example of this as well in the first sentence of Text 2.1: *fatalities caused through the misuse of firearms*. We can re-express this, eliminating the embedding as follows:

Firearms cause fatalities.

Using a preposition this would come out as:

Fatalities occur because of firearms.

And with a conjunction as:

A lot of people die because too many people have firearms.

Note that as we translate the original sentence back towards the typical spoken form, we have to be more explicit about what we mean. *Firearms* turns into *too many people have firearms* and *fatalities becomes A lot of people die*. These additional details do help to clarify the argument. But in writing we do not normally express reasoning in this way.

So far we have seen that reasoning can be signalled by conjunctions, prepositions, and verbs. In fact there is a fourth way to express reasoning, although it is not used in Text 2.1. So let's imagine reorganising Text 2.1 as follows:

I feel that all governments should pass firmer laws on the control of firearms.

There are two reasons for this.

First, it would protect our wildlife.

Second, it would avoid tragic accidents.

There is another example of reasoning with a verb in Text 2.1: *This would cease the hunting and slaughter of our wildlife*. How could this be expressed using a conjunction in place of the verb *cease*?

This time a noun is used to express reasoning: *There are two reasons for this*. Using a conjunction, this version of Text 2.1 would come out as follows:

I feel that all governments should pass firmer laws on the control of firearms because it would protect wildlife and avoid tragic accidents.

We can see from this that reasoning nouns help to organise the arguments in Exposition. This might be especially important if the arguments are more than a clause or two long. If we spent a paragraph discussing the danger firearms pose for wildlife and another discussing tragic shooting accidents, then reasoning nouns would be almost essential to introduce and keep track of the arguments. So in one sense, reasoning with nouns helps us to be clear.

Reasoning in speech and in writing are very different.

Reasoning with nouns, verbs, and prepositions is very typical of writing in our culture, especially in Exposition. The writer of Text 2.1 is already well on her way to reasoning in a written way. With other writers, spoken reasoning may predominate, leading to texts like Text 2.2 from Year 10.

Text 2.2   Are Governments necessary? Give reasons for your answer.
I think Governments are necessary because if there wasn't any there would be no law people would be killing themselves. They help keep our economic system in order for certain things. If there wasn't no Federal Government there wouldn't have been no one to fix up any problems that would have occured in the community. Same with the State Government if the SG didn't exist there would have been noone to look after the schools, vandalism, fighting would have occured everyday. The local Government would be important to look after the rubbish because everyone would have diseases. (Year 10)

In this text the reasoning is mainly accomplished through conjunctions:

I think Governments are necessary <u>because</u> if there wasn't any there would be no law . . .

<u>If</u> there wasn't no Federal Government there wouldn't have been no one to fix up any problems . . .

<u>If</u> the SG didn't exist there would have been no one to look after the schools . . .

The local Government would be important to look after the rubbish, <u>because</u> everyone would have diseases.

Prepositions, nouns, and verbs are of course present; but they are not used to reason. Most readers would probably find Text 2.2 a poor example of Exposition. The main reason for this, I would argue, is that it sounds spoken, not written. Throughout, the grammar of spoken English intrudes:

spoken negatives:	If there wasn't no Federal Government (cf. if there wasn't <u>any</u>)
spoken concord:	because if there wasn't any (cf. if there <u>weren't</u> any)
spoken ellipsis:	Same with the State Government (cf. <u>The same is true of</u>)
spoken co-ordination:	vandalism, fighting (cf. vandalism <u>and</u> fighting)

20

The spoken reasoning, with conjunctions marking cause and effect instead of nouns, verbs, and prepositions, is just one aspect of this oral patterning. The way in which other students in the same writing situation began their essays will perhaps help to emphasise the difference between spoken and written reasoning:

There are many <u>reasons</u> for my saying Governments are necessary.

I think that a Government is necessary for many <u>reasons</u>.

By looking at the world today, at each and every country, you will see that all have some form of government, which <u>means</u> that the government must be necessary.

In the first two openings, arguments are introduced with a noun: *reasons*. In the third, the causal link between having governments and needing governments is expressed by the verb *means*. None of the students in this Year 10 geography class were able to develop Expositions in which only nouns, verbs, and prepositions were used to express cause and effect. But some at least started off on the right track.

The best way to understand the way in which reasoning is expressed in expository writing is to take examples from actual texts and re-express them using conjunctions instead of verbs, prepositions instead of nouns, and so on. Most people are surprised when they do this to discover just how inexplicit reasoning is in mature written Exposition. We will try and interpret the reasons for this in Chapter 3.

Personality in Exposition

Writing is often characterised as impersonal. What exactly do we mean by this? Again we need to look at the ways in which English can be used to express attitudes and feelings and then look at how these structures are used in Exposition. What then are the typical ways in which English speakers express their subjective reactions?

One way is to talk about one's own feelings—wanting, hoping, fearing, enjoying, hating, liking, and so on. In English there are two typical ways of doing this. One is to use a mental process clause of affection:

I <u>love</u> riding motorcycles/Motorcycles <u>thrill</u> me.

The other is through a set of closely related relational processes:

I <u>was happy</u> that he left.

Another way in which speakers typically express their reactions is by talking about their attitudes. Commonly they use emotive adjectives and nouns to do this—in nominal groups:

that <u>fantastic</u> movie/you <u>idiot</u>

and in relational clauses:

That movie was <u>fantastic</u>/You are an <u>idiot</u>

As well there are a large number of purely expressive items, normally used to exclaim:

Yucch/Uggh/Wow/Cor

Casual conversation is full of feelings and attitudes when compared with writing, as Text 2.3 indicates (expressions of feeling and attitude have been underlined in the text).

Text 2.3

K: Mrs Bowen wasn't too happy.
D: 'You dunderheads!'
K: I made some stupid mistakes.

D: So did I . . . I got um.
K: I thought I did quite well in that till we got it back.
D: That's what I thought.
K: Mm . . . It was a disastrous mess.
D: We're having a rhythm test in music . . . soon.
K: How can you have a rhythm test in music?
D: I don't know.
K: I hope we haven't got that student teacher today.
D: So do I.
K: I'll be sick.
D: She was alright I suppose but she . . .
K: Pah. I got ice block in my hair.
D: [laughs] You should tie it back. What about um Paul goes cough she goes 'There's too much noise over on that side of the room'.
    I don't believe it.
    Very particular.
K: Mmm.
D: She . . . What else did she say?
    Um, something she kept on repeating all the time?
K: 'I'll count you in.'
D: Hey?
K/D: Oh 'I'll count you in'.
K: I hated her.
    I bet you we have her again today.
D: You hated her probably 'cause, Bronwyn said that she looked like you.
K: I was thinking about getting my fringe cut on the weekend.
D: [laughs]
K: That would have pleased her.
D: I wouldn't.
K: Look like her! Yuk!
    I meant to wear my hair in a different way today but I didn't.
D: Oh well, can't help it. She wasn't that bad. (Carr et al. 1984, pp.17–18)

Feelings:	Mrs Bowen wasn't too happy
	I hope we
	I hated her
	You hated her
	That would have pleased her
Attitudes:	You dunderheads
	Stupid mistakes
	did quite well
	a disastrous mess

	she was alright
	very particular
	wasn't that bad
Expressions:	Pah
	Yuk

In writing, expressions like these occur frequently only in quotations. Elsewhere, expressive elements like *Pah* and *Yuk* occur scarcely at all, and the expression of feelings and attitudes is rather restricted. Let's go back now to Text 2.1 and look at the expression of feeling and attitude in that text.

Feelings:	I feel . . .
	The Government are to afraid . . .
Attitudes:	responsible people
	slaughter
	an innocent eighteen year old
	precious
	this tragic way

As far as feelings are concerned, we can see that the writer makes her own feelings explicit just once: *I feel all governments . . .* . The only other explicit mention of feelings relates to the Government: *Government are to afraid*. The writer's attitudes, on the other hand, are much more frequently expressed—four times by adjectives: *responsible*, *innocent*, *precious*, and *tragic*; and once by a noun: *slaughter*. Now let's compare this with the expression of feelings and attitudes in Text 2.2:

Feelings: —

Attitudes: The local Government would be important.

We can see from this comparison that there is in fact a difference in the expression of feelings and attitudes between Hortatory and Analytical Exposition. Exposition which tries to persuade people to do something is more like spoken language—a number of feelings and attitudes are expressed. But in Analytical Exposition, whose function is to persuade people that some judgment is correct, feelings and attitudes hardly occur at all. It is this restriction on the expression of feelings and attitudes which people are referring to when they characterise writing, and Analytical Exposition in particular, as impersonal. Traditional strictures against writing Exposition in the first person are part of this pattern.

Exposition intended to persuade is more like speech than is Analytical Exposition, in which personal attitudes find little expression.

There **are** ways around this. One of the most common is to use nouns instead of verbs or adjectives to express feeling and attitude. In Text 2.1, for example, the writer speaks of *my concern over the fatalities*. Remember that in the spoken version of this, with conjunctions carrying the reasoning, the feeling would have come out as a verb, not a noun:

I am writing because I am concerned.

Try rewriting Text 2.1 using nouns instead of verbs and adjectives to express feelings and attitudes. Does the text now sound more 'written' than before?

Similarly attitudes may be transferred to nouns, as has happened with *slaughter*:

responsible	→	responsibility
innocent	→	innocence
precious	→	great value
tragic	→	tragedy

Turning attitudes into abstract qualities is one way of sounding objective while still presenting a point of view. Analytical Exposition in particular favours such nominalised forms.

We have now observed that, in Exposition, reasoning is less explicit than in speaking, and that there are restrictions on the expression of a writer's own feelings and attitudes. We need to take one more step before bringing these ideas together.

Exposition and metaphor

Let's go back once again to Text 2.2. Suppose we were to ask, from the point of view of the writer of Text 2.2, the question 'What do governments do?'. As far as the first four clauses are concerned, the answer would be one that characterises fairly literally what governments actually do do: they pass laws (or 'enact legislation' if one prefers formal language here)—*if there wasn't any [governments] there would be no law*. In the rest of the text, however, a systematic and revealing change in characterisation occurs. Consider the following:

They help keep our economic system in order . . .

there wouldn't have been no one to fix up any problems . . .

there would have been noone to look after the schools . . .

For the rest of the text, governments are characterised not as organisations that enact legislation but as people (*they*, *no one*, *noone*) who tend to *help*, *fix up*, *look after* the economy, social problems, and schools. Governments, in other words, are being personified as a kind of parent who looks after the community. This metaphor, that governments are like parents, is the vehicle through which the necessity of governments is explained.

Metaphor is typically found in expository writing.

Metaphorical explanations such as these are absolutely typical of expository writing. This is a very important point because metaphor is usually something that teachers associate with poetry and narrative. But in fact it lies at the heart of explanation in factual writing as well. Expository metaphors are rarely realised through simile—that is the poet's tool; the writer of Text 2.2 does not actually say that *Governments are like parents*. But the processes selected to describe what governments do (*help*, *fix up*, *look after*) are clearly chosen to portray governments in this way. One **could** argue that metaphors expressed in this way are less explicit than those created by similes—and this would give us an insight into one of the covert ways in which Exposition interprets the world. But the metaphors are there, nonetheless—an integral feature of factual texts.

24

Reason, personality, and metaphor in Exposition

In the last three sections we have seen that Exposition is highly metaphorical, impersonal, and has a tendency to reason within rather than between clauses. In order to understand why Exposition has developed in this way we need to look again at the function of expository writing in our culture. Why are metaphors used? Why don't authors express their feelings and attitudes? And why is the reasoning buried?

Why are feelings and attitudes not found in expository writing?

As noted earlier, the main function of Exposition in our culture is to explain—if Analytical, to explain why things are as they are; if Hortatory, to explain why they should change. This seems to affect metaphor, impersonality, and reasoning in the following way.

Firstly, metaphor. Clearly if we are going to explain something we cannot just describe it for what it is. In Text 2.2 the writer cannot simply describe in a literal way what governments do—that would be stating the obvious. Expositions are not just Reports or Descriptions. Rather things are explained in order to interpret the world. And metaphors are an effective way of getting beyond the obvious. In Text 2.2 governments are treated as parents. Everybody understands what parents do and why they are necessary. And if governments are parents, they must be necessary too. Of course the argument sounds absurd when spelled out in this way. But did you actually smile at the use of this metaphor when first reading Text 2.2? Probably not. Most likely it quietly added plausibility to Text 2.2. In a subliminal way it may have half convinced you. All expository writing uses metaphor, often insidiously, in this way.

Try spelling out the metaphors in expository texts that irritate you. Can you now see more clearly what was so annoying?

Secondly, impersonality. Expositions are supposed to be rational. And in our culture, reason and emotion are felt to be diametrically opposed. Intellect must not be confused with feeling, and whenever it is we become suspicious. Prime ministers who cry may seem all the more human for doing so—but can they really run the country properly? Can they be trusted to make sensible decisions? For this reason most overt expression of feelings or attitudes in Analytical Exposition is frowned upon; and writers generally remove themselves entirely from the argument by writing in the third person. (In scientific writing, passives may be used to remove people altogether—only reason and facts remain!) Hortatory Exposition is less stringent in this respect. Writing in the first person is common, and attitude is expressed, though less frequently than in casual conversation. The reason for this difference seems to be that Hortatory Exposition is often addressed to a specific rather than a general audience (*I* talking to *you*) and that it is intended to persuade—emotional appeals are just as effective in getting people on side as rational ones, and attitudinal expressions are exploited to this end. In spoken Hortatory texts, reason and emotion are apparently felt to complement, not contradict, each other. So oral Hortatory Exposition will be considerably less impersonal than written Analytical texts.

Hortatory Exposition is often addressed to a specific rather than a general audience.

Finally, reasoning. The main issue here is the vulnerability of one's argumentation. Returning again to Text 2.1 and 2.2, we can see that the reasoning in Text 2.1 is much less explicit than in Text 2.2. Let's look again at part of Text 2.1 where the causal link is realised by a verb:

25

Small firearms should only be issued under a licence to responsible people such as policemen and security guards. Large firearms should only be owned and used by gunclubs and their members. This would cease the hunting and slaughter of our wildlife

Assuming that *this* refers to both preceding sentences, if we rework this into the spoken style of Text 2.2, something like the following would result:

Text 2.4

If small firearms were only issued under licence to responsible people and large firearms were only owned by gunclubs, then people would stop slaughtering our wildlife.

The effect of this change is clear. In Text 2.4 the reason and conclusion are more readily identified; as well, the hypothetical nature of the argument, carried by modality and modulation in Text 2.1 (*should*, *should*, and *would*), is made explicit through the conjunction *if*. So Text 2.4 is both more tentative and more accessible as far as argumentation goes than Text 2.1—possible lines of refutation, picking up on the modalities, are much more clear.

Conversely, we can experiment with strengthening the argument in Text 2.2 by getting rid of its conjunctions. Thus we might rewrite part of Text 2.2 as Text 2.5:

I think Governments are necessary because if there wasn't any there would be no law people would be killing themselves.

Removing conjunctions, we get:

Text 2.5

The main reason for having Governments is this—Governments pass laws which prevent people from killing themselves.

In Text 2.5 the verb *prevent* realises the causal link between passing laws and people killing themselves; and the hypothetical *if* has been removed. In Text 2.5 then an argument is presented not as supposition but as an unassailable fact. In our culture burying the reasoning in this way has the effect of strengthening one's case.

In this section we have seen that metaphor, impersonality, and a buried rationale conspire to make the theses that people present in Exposition more plausible. Now we need to stop for a moment and ask ourselves what kind of culture it is that would evolve expository genres which function in this way. There is no simple answer to this question. But we would not be too far from the mark in saying that such a culture must in some way see Exposition as a quest for truth. People in such a culture believe that there is a reality out there which can be discovered if only we look hard enough. It is the job of Exposition to uncover that reality and to present it to readers. Such an ideology would then try to suppress as far as possible the obvious fact that reality exists only in the eye of the beholder—it doesn't really exist apart from observers' subjective constructions of experience; and these subjective constructions always involve metaphorical interpretation and layers of reasoning

Why does a culture evolve expository genres?

which amount to little more than acts of faith, whatever the science or social science involved. Scientists and social scientists are much less prone than other members of society to think of their theories as true. They tend to view their 'discoveries' as interpretations—the best models they can find to fit most of their observations at a given time. Science fashions perspectives on reality; it is not a quest for truth. All this then has to be covered up in a culture that believes in truth. For this reason the expository conspiracies we have just reviewed must be mastered by children if they are to take their place as mature writers and readers in our culture.

Spoken and written modes

Throughout this chapter reference has been made to differences between speaking and writing. So in this concluding section, two of these differences which are particularly relevant to Exposition will be briefly reviewed.

Complexity: density and intricacy

Many people have the mistaken idea that speaking is simpler than writing, and that this is one reason writing is hard to learn. In fact both speech and writing make use of complex linguistic patterns, although the complexity tends to be of different kinds. The complexity of speaking is grammatical—very long sentences may well be produced once speakers depart from the rapid-fire repartee of texts like Text 2.3 and take a longer turn, with clause added to clause in a complex array. Consider, for example, the following text, taken from an interview with the author of this book:

Differences between speech and writing are discussed in detail by Halliday in Spoken and Written Language *(1989).*

Text 2.6
1			This [i.e. genre] is a literary term,
⁺2			but you extend it
ˣ3			so it's not only what a poem is, or an essay,
⁺4	1	α	but a service encounter
		⁼β	(as when you go into a shop)—
	⁼2		something you would have to define with respect to mode and field and tenor,
⁺5	⁺β		and rather than wrangle any more with linguists about what functional tenor is,
	α	1	I gave up the term
		⁺2	and developed the term genre for this underlying set of things.

The grammatical relationship between the clauses in Text 2.6 is shown, following Halliday (1985). Greek letters are used to relate clauses if they are dependent on each other; numerals, if they are co-ordinated or in apposition. The ⁼ sign refers to ELABORATION (*that is, for example*); the ⁺ sign, to EXTENSION (*and, or*); the ˣ sign, to ENHANCEMENT (cause and time); and the ' sign, to a PROJECTED IDEA (reporting thoughts and feelings).

In writing, on the other hand, the complexity is lexical—large numbers of content words are typically packed into a single clause, making each clause a mouthful to consume; grammatical relations between clauses in writing are usually very simple.

Because writing is very prestigious in our culture (most people's views on language are in fact views on written, not spoken, language), and valued over speech, mature adult speakers are often influenced by writing in the way they talk. On many public occasions, spoken language may be very influenced by writing indeed. Important people talk like books—this makes them seem important. So the language of sermons, political interviews, lectures, and the like tends to pattern like writing: it is grammatically simple and lexically complex. This is one reason why many lecturers are so hesitant in their oral presentations.

When young children are learning to write, the interaction of speech and writing is just the opposite—instead of writing influencing speaking, young children write as they talk. Text 2.2 is a good example of writing influenced in this way from a writer who is still having problems moving into the written mode even after many years of writing. Compared to Text 2.1, Text 2.2 is grammatically complex—or INTRICATE as Halliday (1989) refers to it in *Spoken and Written Language*; but lexically it is much more diffuse than Text 2.1—DENSITY is Halliday's term for complexity of this kind. Let's now look at Text 2.1 and Text 2.2 from this point of view to see the different kinds of complexity involved.

By comparing Figure 2.1 with Figure 2.2, we can see the degree to which Text 2.2 is influenced by speaking as far as its grammatical complexity is concerned. Its sentences are far more intricate than those in Text 2.1.

Figure 2.1 Clause complex relations in Text 2.1

I am <u>writing</u> because of my <u>concern</u> over the <u>fatalities</u> <u>caused</u> through the <u>misuse</u> of <u>firearms</u>.	(6)
α I <u>feel</u>	(1)
'β all <u>governments</u> should <u>pass</u> <u>firmer</u> <u>laws</u> on the <u>control</u> of <u>firearms</u>.	(6)
<u>Small</u> <u>firearms</u> should only be <u>issued</u> under a <u>license</u> to <u>responsible</u> <u>people</u> such as <u>policemen</u> and <u>security</u> <u>guards</u>.	(9)
<u>Large</u> <u>firearms</u> should only be <u>owned</u> and <u>used</u> by <u>gunclubs</u> and their <u>members</u>.	(6)
This would <u>cease</u> the <u>hunting</u> and <u>slaughter</u> of our <u>wildlife</u>.	(4)
<u>Recent</u> <u>examples</u> of <u>firearm</u> <u>accidents</u> are—<u>Ronald</u> <u>Reagan's</u> <u>attempted</u> <u>assassination</u>, an <u>innocent</u> <u>eighteen</u> <u>year</u> <u>old</u> <u>shot</u> by an <u>angry</u> <u>boyfriend</u> and a <u>six</u> <u>year</u> <u>old</u> <u>boy</u> <u>killed</u> while <u>playing</u> with a <u>gun</u> at a <u>friends</u> house.	(24)
The <u>Government</u> are to <u>afraid</u> of <u>losing</u> their <u>place</u> because of the <u>communities</u> <u>opinions</u> of <u>firearms</u>.	(7)
α <u>Life</u> is to <u>precious</u>	(2)
×β to be <u>lost</u> in this <u>tragic</u> way.	(3)

Text 2.1 consists of eight sentences; only two of these are clause complexes—the rest are simple sentences. But Text 2.2, on the other hand, has five sentences; only one of which is not a clause complex—

Figure 2.2 Clause complex relations in Text 2.2

α	α		I <u>think</u>	(1)
	'β		<u>Governments</u> are necessary	(1)
×β	×β		because if there wasn't any	(-)
	α	1	there would be no <u>law</u>	(1)
		×2	<u>people</u> would be <u>killing</u> themselves.	(2)
			They <u>help</u> <u>keep</u> our <u>economic</u> <u>system</u> in <u>order</u> for certain things.	(6)
	×β		If there wasn't no <u>Federal</u> <u>Government</u>	(2)
	α	α	there wouldn't have been no one	(-)
		×β	to <u>fix up</u> any <u>problems</u> that would have <u>occured</u> in the <u>community</u>.	(4)
1			Same with the State Government	(2)
=2	×β		if the <u>SG</u> didn't <u>exist</u>	(2)
	α	α	there would have been noone	(-)
	×β	1	to <u>look after</u> the <u>schools</u>	(2)
		×2	<u>vandalism</u>, <u>fighting</u> would have <u>occured</u> everyday.	(3)
	α		The <u>local</u> <u>Government</u> would be <u>important</u>	(3)
	×β		to <u>look after</u> the <u>rubbish</u>	(2)
	×γ		because everyone would have <u>diseases</u>.	(1)

and the clause complexes themselves are rather complex: two have 5 clauses, two have 3 clauses, and one consists of only a single clause. What we are really looking at here is the effect of burying the reasoning in written Exposition. In speaking, argumentation is carried along by the clause complex, with links made explicit through conjunctions. In writing, the reasoning is submerged, realised within rather than between clauses.

What about lexical density? This can be calculated by counting up the lexical items in each of the clauses in Figure 2.1 and Figure 2.2. In doing this we will ignore function words: pronouns, auxiliary verbs, prepositions, conjunctions, and other closed system items such as *everyday*—these words are really part of the grammar and need to be passed over here. The lexical items, or content words, in each clause have been underlined and totalled at the end of each clause in Figures 2.1 and 2.2. By dividing the number of lexical items by the number of clauses we can get a measure of the lexical density of each text. Text 2.2 turns out to have about 2 lexical items per clause, while Text 2.1 has 6.8. So Text 2.1 is more than three times as dense lexically as Text 2.2. This kind of difference in lexical density is typical of the difference between speaking and writing. Mature written texts will be much less diffuse than Text 2.2.

What is the lexical density of Text 2.3, the conversation looked at above?

Grammatical metaphor

In the previous section we dispelled the myth that writing is more complex than speaking, at least in one important respect. What about another of the prevailing myths about language complexity in our culture—namely that children's language is simple and direct? In one respect this too is wrong. The six-year-old speaker of Text 2.7 makes use of clause complex structures that are far from simple. But in another sense, children's language is simple. In order to interpret this simplicity we need to introduce the concept of grammatical metaphor, which in fact we have already been dealing with for some time.

Text 2.7   Spoken clause complex by six-year-old

1	α	Well, I quit early
	×β	because it's a little too much
	×γ 1	because I have to take piano
	+2	and I'd have to go there
+2	α	and, you know, it's a little bit too much for me
	×β	because I have to practise
	×γ	when I get home.

When we were unpacking the reasoning in Text 2.1, we were in effect making use of the concept of grammatical metaphor. So let's look once again at the opening sentence in Text 2.1: *I am writing because of my concern over the fatalities caused through the misuse of firearms*. In English, as in all languages, there is an unmarked relation between meanings and forms. Unless there is a good reason for not doing so, we use nouns to code people, places, and things, verbs to code actions, and conjunctions to code relations between clauses. But what about this opening sentence from Text 2.1?

An unmarked feature of language is a typical and therefore 'unremarkable' feature.

Figure 2.3   The relation between forms and meanings in the first sentence of Text 2.1

	form	meaning
I	noun	person (Actor)
writing	verb	action
my	pronoun	person (Senser)
concern	noun	feeling
fatalities	noun	quality
caused	verb	causal relation
misuse	noun	action
firearms	noun	thing

As Figure 2.3 shows, some of the meanings in the opening of Text 2.1 are being coded in an unmarked way: the writer comes out as a person (*I*), her act of writing as a verb (*writing*), and firearms come out as a noun (*firearms*). But elsewhere the relation of meaning to form seems out of step. The feeling of 'being concerned' and the action of 'misusing firearms' come out as nouns: *concern* and *misuse*; the person who feels the feeling comes out as a possessive pronoun (*my*) modifying *concern*, not as a Senser; the causal connection between fatalities and misusing firearms comes out as a verb (*caused*) not as a conjunction; and the quality 'fatal' comes out as a personified abstraction (*fatalities*). Text 2.1 is full of mismatches of this kind as we have seen. This incongruence between meaning and form is referred to by Halliday (1985) as GRAMMATICAL METAPHOR. The function of the majority of metaphors of this kind in English is to turn things that we expect to come out as verbs, prepositions, adjectives, conjunctions, and modals into nouns. This process is referred to as nominalisation.

If we take the grammatical metaphors out of the opening section of Text 2.1 we get a text something like the following:

Text 2.8
I am writing
because I am concerned
that people are misusing firearms
and thereby fatally wounding lots of people.

Note how the argumentation surfaces as the metaphors are unpacked. Of course the effect of this is to turn writing into speaking, and at the same time to make the language more childlike. When speaking, children do not appear to make much use of grammatical metaphor until about nine years of age. And grammatical metaphor seems to come into their writing a little later than this. In order to mature as writers, children must learn to make extensive use of grammatical metaphor. If they don't, their writing will sound immature. This is one of the problems with Text 2.2. The only real nominalisations in Text 2.2 are *vandalism* and *fighting*; Text 2.1 on the other hand is packed with metaphor from start to finish. This may be the time to ask yourself how you reacted when you first read Text 2.2. To what extent did you try and explain your negative reactions in terms of the 'incorrect' grammar of the text (the incursions of spoken language into written English, in other words)? Can you decide now what was actually influencing your judgment?

How many examples of grammatical metaphor can you find?

There are other grammatical metaphors which have to do with MOOD and MODALITY rather than meaning about people, things, actions, qualities, and logical relations. There is an example of this kind of metaphor near the beginning of Text 2.1: *I feel all governments should pass firmer laws on the control of firearms*. The surface grammar of this sentence is that of a statement—a kind of clause that gives information. But the sentence is really a Command. The writer is really telling governments what to do. The unmarked form of this meaning would be an imperative: *Pass firmer laws on the control of firearms*. But in Exposition, direct imperatives are avoided. For one thing, the people who are supposed to respond to the request may not be people at all but an organisation and so too abstracted to refer to as *you*, the understood Subject of a direct imperative. For another, direct requests for action are too subjective. They reflect too clearly the writer's own desires and needs. Modulations of obligation and necessity such as *should* help to turn direct requests into more 'objective' assertions of obligation—they appeal to right and wrong, to some higher moral authority, and thus disguise the subjectivity of the writer's own preferences. Here we are arguing in other words that *You should pass firmer laws* is more objective than *Pass firmer laws*, and that *Firmer laws are necessary* is more objective again.

Similarly, with modality, which is typically realised in the verbal group (*we may go*, *we must go*, etc.), impersonal expressions are preferred in writing. In Text 2.2 the text begins: *I think Governments are necessary*, with the modulation of necessity realised as an adjective. In speaking we would be more likely to say *I think we should have governments*, with the necessity as a verb (*should*). The spoken form makes the source of the necessity clear: it comes from the writer/speaker. And it makes the necessity more accessible to debate. The first

31

part of the verbal group is the bit we throw back and forth in arguing: *We should have Governments.—No, we shouldn't.—Yes, we should. We must have them.* With *Governments are necessary* the debate turns into a question of 'yes' or 'no' (*—No, they aren't. —Yes they are. — They are not. —They are too.*) oriented to the truth or falsity of the proposition; the source of the judgments as to what is in fact the case is obscured.

Interpersonal metaphors add to a text's objectivity.

Just as the experiential metaphors described earlier help make a text more factual by obscuring its reasoning, so interpersonal metaphors like these add to a text's objectivity. Requests for action come out as statements. Assessments of obligation and possibility come out as facts. Through all of this, the voice of the writer disappears. He becomes a recorder of reality, a purveyor of truth. The text is presented as given, not an **interpretation** of what is.

Grammatical metaphor is at the heart of the linguistic conspiracies described in the previous section. Children need to learn to read texts which are full of grammatical metaphors if they are to access the information contained in them. Children need to learn to produce grammatical metaphors if they are to write convincing Expositions. And most important, children need to learn **about** grammatical metaphors if they are to defend themselves from perverse ideologies masquerading as fact and truth. In Chapter 3, we will look at the ways in which adults use Exposition, to get an idea of just how important this kind of knowledge about language turns out to be.

Chapter 3

Challenging social reality: Hortatory and Analytical Exposition in adult writing

What then of adults? What do the few students who actually do master Exposition do with it when they grow up? In a book such as this we can really do no more than illustrate one of the uses of Exposition, with examples taken from a particular ideological context. We will follow on from Chapter 2 by analysing one Hortatory and one Analytical Expository text. The Thesis of the Hortatory text is that Australia should stop killing kangaroos; the Thesis of the Analytical text is that Canada is harvesting seal pups in a responsible way. Although the texts are taken from two different debates, the environmental and moral issues involved are so similar that the texts seem almost to be arguing against each other. This then will be the context of our discussion: two texts, one challenging, one defending, the status quo.

Ideology in crisis

At present in schools, most children work in make-believe contexts. Analytical Exposition is mainly used to demonstrate that content has been learned; it is not usually used to analyse and interpret the world in new ways. Hortatory Exposition is used in mock debates concerning issues that crop up in social science or history; it is rarely used to challenge the structure of the world outside the classroom (still less is it used to challenge the nature of schooling itself!). In some schools Exposition is sometimes used in adult ways, as part of general studies programs, for example, that focus on ecology or peace studies; but these programs are not yet widespread (interestingly enough, in spite of their limited scope, such programs may lead to hysterical outbursts such as Greg Sheridan's 'The lies they teach our children' in the *Weekend Australian*, 2–3 Feb., 1985, which charges that children using language in this way have to been fed on a 'diet of intellectual poison' which is 'hostile to Australia, to the US, to capitalism, to European civilisation, to industry, to Christianity'. These restrictions have little to do with children's writing abilities; but they do have very much to do with the nature of schooling and the use it makes of Exposition in its daily practice.

For adults, on the other hand, Exposition is for real. It is used to interpret the world in new ways (in science and social science, for example), and it is used to challenge existing social orders (in politics, for example). So in order to really understand the function of Exposition in our culture and why it uses language in the way it does, we have to leave schools as they are presently conceived, and look at adults' writing.

In doing this we must become more explicit about the relationship between language and ideology than we have been to this point—because the function of Exposition cannot be appreciated without taking the ideology of a culture into account. In one sense, this is a difficult step. Ideology is pervasive in every culture, but like most other types of meaning it is largely unconscious. And while linguists have been studying language for centuries, it is only recently that they have turned their attention to the ideology that language encodes. To make things easier, here in Chapter 3, we will look at what happens when the social order is challenged—ideology in crisis is much easier to observe than ideology which is unconsciously accepted as just the way things are. Then in Chapter 4, we will move back to looking at writing in schools, and try to investigate the latent, unchallenged ideology that underlies the kinds of writing children do and the way writing is not taught.

We will note in passing a number of ways in which this latent ideology should be challenged. But to date it is not in anything like the kind of crisis we will be exploring in this chapter.

One way of identifying ideological crises is to frame them as questions. Some Australian examples would include:

Should Australia mine and export uranium?
Should New Zealand allow nuclear warships into its ports?
Should pornographic videos be censored?
Should women be allowed to commemorate women raped in war on Anzac Day?
Should creationism be taught in schools?
Should rain forests be logged or harmed in any way?
Should land rights be given to Aborigines?
Should Australia accept fewer Asian migrants?

Clearly this list could be extended. Equally clearly crises come and go. Most of these issues would have been unthinkable a hundred years ago—not that Australia was not a racist, sexist, Christian, and capitalist country then as it is now. But a hundred years ago racism, for example, was latent ideology. Few challenged it. And certainly there was no question of society being restructured because of such a challenge.

Ideology has primarily to do with power. Whenever ideology is challenged, the way in which power is shared by a community comes under attack. As this happens, groups whose share in power is implicated by the crisis align themselves. All of this has the effect of making the ideological basis of power much more clear.

Take, for example, the question of whether Australia should mine and export uranium. This issue, as phrased, has two **sides**, for and against. Treating **issues** as ideological systems, we arrive at the picture in Figure 3.1.

Figure 3.1 Issues and sides in the uranium debate

ISSUE: should Australia mine and export uranium? ——→ ⌈ SIDE: for

                                                               ⌊ SIDE: against

Now that we have introduced the idea of issues and sides, at least as this linguist construes them, let's take another step by noting that most debates involve people of two kinds. Firstly there are the stirrers. These are the so-called radicals of the Left and conservatives of the Right who see their job as that of creating issues. They seize upon some latent aspect of ideology, and force it out into the conscious public domain. Secondly there are the resolvers. Their job is to make issues go away by working out some kind of compromise. We will refer to the stirrers as ANTAGONISTS and the resolvers as PROTAGONISTS. Taking this step into account, and providing examples of the kinds of groups involved, we can develop Figure 3.1 into Figure 3.2

Figure 3.2 Antagonists and protagonists in the uranium debate

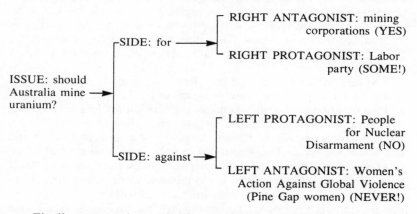

Finally we need to take into account the question of power. Ideology has to do with the distribution of power in a culture; as noted above, when ideology is challenged, the way in which power is shared in a society is questioned. In Western capitalist societies, power resides principally with those who control the means of production and the knowledge needed to effect that control. Traditionally, groups holding this power are referred to as 'the **Right**', and those challenging their power as 'the **Left**'. To simplify matters we will simply adopt these terms here. The Right then refers to people who have power to lose when ideology is challenged and the Left, to people who have power to gain. The terms Right and Left have already been included in Figure 3.2. It should perhaps be stressed here that when we refer to the Labor Party as the Right protagonist in the uranium debate we are not implying that this party always functions in that role; this is simply the role they are currently playing in this debate. Before their election to government, for example, they played the role of the Left protagonist. Or to take a more striking example, the Festival of Light and radical feminist organisations play the same role in debates about pornography when with respect to almost every other issue they are Right and Left antagonists respectively.

So far then we have introduced the following terms:

issues	a way of formulating challenges to an ideological system
sides	the way in which people align themselves with respect to an issue
antagonists	people who create issues
protagonists	people who resolve issues
Right	people who have power to lose
Left	people who have power to gain

Reviewing then, issues arise when ideology is challenged. These challenges are initiated by antagonists. Left antagonists include feminist activists, land rights activists, gay rights organisations, Greenpeace, various Marxist organisations, Doctors Reform Society, and so on. Their job is to challenge the power traditionally held by the Right. Right antagonists include the Festival of Light, the National Front, the National Party, fundamentalist religious groups, large capitalist corporations, etc. Their function is to regain power which has devolved to the Left, i.e. away from its traditional owners. In the middle, as it were, are the protagonists. Their function is to redistribute power, from the Right to the Left or back again, depending on political expediency.

At this point some of you may feel I am using the term 'power' in a peculiar way. Is the issue of abortion on demand, for example, really a question of power, you might ask? Isn't it really a moral issue, having to do with conscience, morality, and religious belief? To this I would have to answer that this is simply the way people dress up and talk about the issue. The Right, for example, tends to treat abortion as an ethical question, rather than a debate about who controls women's lives. They are of course free to do this and to present their case in moral terms. But treating the question as an ethical one does not mean that power is not involved. To see this, all we have to do is ask who gains and who loses if women are forced to have children every time they become pregnant. Men gain power, because women have to interrupt careers and give up jobs; this generally makes them less competitive in employment and usually materially dependent on men when they stop work. The Church gains power, because priests and ministers rather than women decide whether or not a pregnancy will be terminated. The Right in general gains power, because its women are better at avoiding pregnancy than working-class or migrant women, and so avoid the disadvantages of large numbers of young children to mind. This analysis could certainly be extended. But the point I am trying to make here is that however you look at the issue, power is clearly involved. And the groups that oppose abortion are essentially those that have power to lose; while those in favour of abortion have power to gain.

Ideology and genre

Ideology and genre are intimately related in any culture, from both the perspective of latent ideology and the challenges to ideology which are under focus in this part of the book. As far as latent ideology is concerned, one good measure of the way in which power is distributed is to ask how many and which genres different groups in society have access to. Illiterate people, for example, do not have access to any of the written genres in our culture. This puts them at a tremendous disadvantage, making them dependent on readers and writers in countless ways. Similarly, children have access to far fewer genres than adults. This is not just a question of inexperience. Many genres, including religious ceremonies, participation in political processes, marriage, and so on are actually proscribed for this group.

When ideology is challenged, genre becomes implicated in another way. Here it is not so much a question of which genres a group is able to use, but which genres a group **chooses** to use to make its case. Antagonists, for example, favour genres which attract the attention of the media. Political marches and rallies, sit-ins, pamphlets, graffiti, sabotage, kidnapping, and hijacking are all exploited by antagonists to make people aware of issues they are trying to promote. Unfortunately we don't have time to explore antagonists' genres in this book. Instead we will concentrate on two of the genres commonly used by protagonists.

To begin, we need a model of the issues underlying the texts we are going to examine. The Canadian issue is modelled in Figure 3.3, the Australian one, in Figure 3.4. As noted above, the issues are very closely related; they are generalised in Figure 3.5.

Figure 3.3 Opposition profile for the Canadian sealing issue

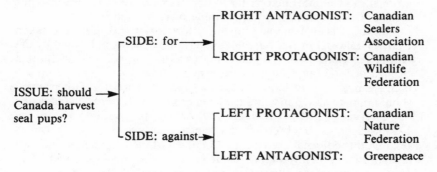

Figure 3.4 Opposition profile for the Australian kangaroo killing issue

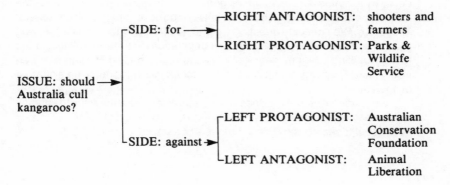

Figure 3.5   Generalising the oppositions in ecological debates

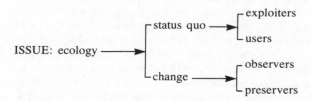

The protagonists in ecological debates tend to favour different genres to present their case. The Left protagonists, or the observers of Figure 3.5, often make use of Hortatory Exposition in a number of modes: editorials, letters to the editor, letters to government officials and politicians, and public speeches. Hortatory Exposition is designed to persuade people **to** do something.

This is a useful genre for the Left protagonists who are trying to change the status quo. Right protagonists, or users, on the other hand tend to favour Analytical Exposition; their editorials, letters, speeches, and articles try to persuade people **that** the status quo is OK—nothing needs to be changed. Analytical Exposition is a useful way of defending the way things are. It presents what already happens as given, correct, and hard to challenge or change. Both groups find the genre favoured by the other exasperating. The Left protagonists find the users' texts cold, scientific, and insensitive to the feelings a particular issue may arouse; the Right protagonists find the observers' texts emotional, irrational, and uninformed as far as the 'facts of the matter' are concerned. Let's look now at an example of each kind of text.

Text 3.1 is an example of mature Hortatory Exposition. It is taken from an editorial in *Habitat* (June 1983), a magazine published by the Australian Conservation Foundation (ACF). The editorial is entitled 'Kangaroos—is our national conscience extinct?' and argues that too many kangaroos are being killed and that at worst the Government should initiate an inquiry into the level of killing. *Habitat*, 'a magazine of conservation and environment', typically expresses the views of the Left protagonists, or observers, in ecological debates. Some of its readers felt that this editorial used a little too much of the language of the Left antagonists for their liking, as letters in succeeding issues showed. Only an excerpt from the editorial is presented here.

Text 3.1   Kangaroos—is our national conscience extinct?

Let us try to define our conservation goals—but on two levels. First comes the level of species survival on which our rather smug government biologists prefer to operate. We seriously question what is happening under their approving eyes: the massive level of killing, the population distortions related to the favoured killing of bigger, heavier male kangaroos, the pathetic lack of supervisory staff. The programme is unsatisfactory and questionable on a number of counts.

Secondly, let us turn to a deeper level: that web of life embracing the human species as well as the easy, trusting targets in the night spotlights. We are talking here about 'deep ecology', about the ethics related to all wild creatures. We don't feel the need to apologise for looking beyond the figures on 'harvests', 'quotas' and 'management' to think for a moment about 3 million other living creatures whose lives will be obliterated, often painfully, this year.

We are in good company. In November 1785, the great poet with the human touch, Robert Burns, wrote a famous poem 'To a Mouse'. . . on turning her up in her nest with the plough. . .

'I'm truly sorry man's dominion
Has broken Nature's social union,
An' justifies that ill opinion
Which makes thee startle
At me, thy poor, earth-born companion
An' fellow mortal!' Burns wrote.
'But Mousie, thou art no thy lane [alone]
In proving foresight may be vain;
The best-laid schemes o' mice an' men
Gang aft agley [askew]
An' lea'e us nought but grief an' pain
For promis'd joy!'

What men and women would we be if we did not care for the lives and suffering of our fellow creatures.

'A dog starved at his master's gate
Predicts the ruin of the state.' wrote the English 'seer' William Blake.
'The wild deer wandering here and there
Keep the human soul from care . . .'

We may not be able to cost out our feeling for our fellow-creatures or the value we place on their wildness and freedom in statistics or export dollars. But we have it. And it is not a lesser thing than aerial population counts or skin prices or that narrower view which measures survival in species and ignores the imposed death of millions.

'For the tear is an intellectual thing', Blake wrote. 'And a sigh is the sword of an Angel King . . .'

So it's still relevant to conservation when we consider: What will killing 3 million kangaroos a year do to us as human beings? What sort of Australians can shrug off that kind of brutality? And what are the implications for the rest of nature, for the bush, for the land, for other animals, for our fellow human beings, when our prime wildlife is killed on this scale? In the end we are talking about our own perception of ourselves as Australians. Our nationhood, our identity, our national pride and self-respect. Our humanity.

Text 3.2 is an example of mature Analytical Exposition. It is taken from *International Wildlife* (March−April 1983), a magazine sponsored by the National Wildlife Federation (NWF) and the Canadian Wildlife Federation (CWF). The article is entitled 'The Northwest Atlantic sealing controversy' and aims to present the facts about sealing so that Federation members can make up their own minds about the killing of baby seals. *International Wildlife*, 'dedicated to the wise use of the earth's resources', typically represents the views of the Right protagonists, or users, in ecological debates. Again, just a part of their article is presented here.

Text 3.2   The North-west Atlantic sealing controversy

Is the clubbing of seals humane?
The answer to that question is unequivocally **Yes**. Observers from humane organizations and veterinary pathologists visit the Canadian sealing operations each year, to observe killing techniques and perform autopsies on seals. Their reports are available to the public and indicate that the whitecoat harvest, which has attracted so much publicity, is conducted in a humane manner.

There is no aesthetically pleasant way to kill an animal, and it may be particularly unpleasant for those who have never seen the slaughter of animals. However, it is necessary to recognize that the East Coast seal hunt is a slaughtering operation, and there is no way that it can be made a pretty sight. It is however, neither cruel nor a massacre. Statements to that effect are false and misleading, designed to generate an emotional response to an otherwise normal operation.

Killing methods, employed by Canadian sealers, are designed to cause an almost instantaneous death, and have been approved by the Canadian Federation of Humane Societies and the Canadian Council on Animal Care. The definition of a humane death is one **where the animal is instantly and irreversibly rendered unconscious resulting in a rapid death, with an absolute minimum of pain or psychological stress.** Methods employed in the seal hunt meet this criteria, and are used by Canada, the USA, the USSR and other countries. The method is considered to be as good as, or superior to, those employed in the slaughter of domestic animals in North America and Europe.

There is little doubt that television coverage of a domestic slaughtering operation, conducted in a government approved abbatoir, which involved the slaughter of lambs, calves and swine, would generate a great deal of public revulsion and protest. Yet the television media have persisted in presenting the seal slaughtering operation as a sensational news item, without considering the usual moral constraints that would apply to the coverage of such an event. It is necessary to question how the media can justify the application of this double standard. Is this because seals are a national resource, or has the media naively permitted itself to be manipulated by opponents of the seal hunt?

The two extracts considered as Texts 3.1 and Text 3.2 deal with theses that are in fact the antithesis of each other. *Habitat* argues that the killing of kangaroos is inhumane; *International Wildlife* argues that the harvesting of whitecoats is as humane as possible. But the ways in which each magazine goes about making its case are very different. Let's now look at the most important of these differences. Overall we will see that the Hortatory text is more personal: it is about people and their feelings and attitudes. The Analytical text is on the other hand impersonal: it deals with facts—the way the world is according to the experts. I have analysed all of the editorial and article from which Text 3.1 (hereafter the ACF text) and Text 3.2 (hereafter the CWF text) are taken and the patterns discussed here are representative of the texts as a whole.

Differences between the Hortatory and Analytical texts

Reference to people

The ACF text refers to people (not simply organisations like the ACF and CWF) twice as often as the CWF text. A little over half the time it makes use of first person pronouns (*we* and *our*) to do so. As well the ACF text refers to individuals by name (e.g. Burns and Blake in Text 3.1).

The CWF text is written in the third person and uses the first person only twice (at the beginning of the article from which Text 3.2 is taken). Many of its references to people are to people as professional experts (e.g. *observers* and *veterinary pathologists* in Text 3.2).

On top of this the ACF text overall uses first position in the clause, or Theme, to refer to people three times as often as the CWF text. A majority of the clauses in Text 3.1 begin in this way. First position in the clause is important in English because it signals what a sentence will be about. And this has the effect of making people much more focal than facts and things in the ACF text; in the CWF text the reverse is true. (Have a look at the initial nouns in clauses in Text 3.1 and Text 3.2; how many are people in each text?)

Verbs of perceiving, feeling, thinking, and saying

Overall the ACF editorial refers to perceiving, feeling, thinking, and saying about three times as often as the CWF article. The CWF article avoids verbs of feeling (wanting, hoping, fearing, etc.), and when it uses a verb of saying, it is often data or reports that talk, not people (e.g. *Their reports indicate that* . . . in Text 3.2). This difference between Texts 3.1 and 3.2 is outlined in Figure 3.6. So not only does the ACF editorial refer to people more often, but it also refers more often to the kinds of things that only people do. The CWF article is more concerned with processes that happen in the world, not in people's heads (e.g. visiting, killing, generating, etc.) or descriptions of the way things are (e.g. *Their reports as available* . . .; *It may be particularly unpleasant* . . .).

Figure 3.6 Processes of perceiving, feeling, thinking, and saying in Texts 3.1 and 3.2.

	ACF—Text 3.1	CWF—Text 3.2
perceiving	—	observe, see
feeling	feel, care	—
thinking	think, ignore, consider	recognise, consider, consider
saying	question, analyse write, write, talk, talk	indicate

Frequency of passives

The ACF editorial uses about half as many passives as the CWF text. This is one way in which the CWF text avoids referring to people as often as the ACF text does. For example, by writing that *The whitecoat harvest . . . is conducted in a humane manner*, the CWF text avoids mentioning the sealers who are involved in the seal hunt. Passives are also used to draw attention away from the 'active' nature of some processes. For example, the CWF text writes: *Killing methods are designed to cause an almost instantaneous death*. Compare this with

(X) <u>has designed</u> killing methods to cause an almost instantaneous death.

The passive *are designed* presents designing as a kind of state, a *fait accompli*; whereas the active *has designed* focuses attention on the activity of designing itself. Stative passives of this kind lend an air of authority and factuality to Analytical Exposition.

Lexical density in the Theme

In Chapter 2 we looked at the question of lexical density and saw that written texts typically have many more lexical items per clause than spoken ones. While the ACF text has a higher lexical density than most spoken language, it is much less complex in this way than Text 3.2.

Figure 3.7   Topical Themes in Texts 3.1 and 3.2; lexical items underlined

ACF—Text 3.1	CWF—Text 3.2
us	the answer to that <u>question</u>
<u>comes</u>	<u>observers</u> from <u>humane</u> <u>organisations</u> and
we	<u>veterinary</u> <u>pathologists</u>
the <u>program</u>	their <u>reports</u>
us	there
we	it
we	it
we	there
In <u>November</u>	it
<u>1785</u>	<u>statements</u> to that <u>effect</u>
<u>poem</u>	<u>killing</u> <u>methods</u>, <u>employed</u> by <u>Canadian</u> <u>sealers</u>,
what <u>men</u> and <u>women</u>	the <u>definition</u> of a <u>humane</u> death
(<u>poem</u>)	<u>methods</u> <u>employed</u> in the <u>seal</u> <u>hunt</u>
we	the <u>method</u>
we	there
it	the <u>television</u> <u>media</u>
(<u>poem</u>)	it
it	this
What	the <u>media</u>
What sort of	
<u>Australians</u>	
What	
we	
Our <u>nationhood</u>	

How many passives can you find in Texts 3.1 and 3.2? How many of these are missing actors that would have appeared in the active? How many are stative passives of the kind just discussed? What are the differences between Texts 3.1 and 3.2 in these respects?

One way to see this is to compare the lexical density of the Themes in the ACF text with those in the CWF text, which has about twice as many lexical items per Theme. This difference in lexical density reflects the more informative and grammatically metaphorical nature of Analytical Exposition. The purpose of the CWF text is to inform, and it packs more lexical information into each clause than the ACF text. Compare the Themes from Texts 3.1 and 3.2 shown in Figure 3.7.

What is the average lexical density of the ACF and CWF Themes?

Experiential metaphor: congruence in the two texts

In Chapter 2 we also looked at the question of congruence, asking, for example, whether actions were being expressed in nouns or verbs. Following this up in Texts 3.1 and 3.2 we can see a big difference in the way in which actions are realised. Overall the CWF article realises actions as nouns twice as often as the ACF editorial.

The CWF article uses three types of nominal structure in place of verbs to realise actions. One puts the action into the modifier of an abstract noun: e.g. *sealing operation*, *killing techniques*. Another makes use of a nominalised form of a verb: *statements*, *definition*, *death*, *coverage*, *constraints*. A third simply realises the actions as a noun: *the whitecoat harvest*, *the East Coast seal hunt*, *the seal hunt*.

Of particular interest is the way in which the two texts refer to the killing of seals and kangaroos. The ACF tends to refer to the killing congruently, as a process: *the massive level of killing*; *the favoured killing of bigger, heavier male kangaroos*; *whose lives will be obliterated*; *killing 3 million kangaroos a year*; *when our prime wildlife is killed on this scale*. The CWF text on the other hand tends to refer to the killing indirectly, using incongruent forms: *killing techniques*, *the whitecoat harvest*, *the slaughter of animals*, *the East Coast seal hunt*, *a slaughtering operation*, *killing methods*, *an almost instantaneous death*, *a humane death*, *the seal hunt*, and so on. In this way the ACF text focuses on the process of killing, while the CWF text treats the killing as a kind of thing. This has the effect of immobilising the most unsavoury part of the seal hunt and helps draw attention away to other 'factual' considerations.

How many of these incongruent realisations of actions can you find in Texts 3.1 and 3.2? How many more nominal realisations of actions does the CWF use?

Statements, suggestions, and questions

So far we have looked at the ways in which the ACF text is more people oriented and active than the CWF text. One further aspect of this is the way in which the ACF text talks to and involves the reader while the CWF text simply presents information in a much less interactive way. Here we are interested in the use of suggestions and questions as opposed to statements in the two texts.

As noted above, the ACF text is written in the first person. This allows it to make suggestions involving the reader as it moves from one stage of the discussion to another:

<u>Let us</u> try and define our conservation goals—but on two levels.

Secondly, <u>let us</u> turn to a deeper level:

Have suggestions been used in a similar way in this book?

This has the effect of involving the reader in the text's development in a way the CWF text does not attempt. In fact throughout the ACF text it is unclear whether the pronouns *we* and *our* refer to the editors or to the editors and readers as well. This systematic ambiguity helps personalise the ACF text.

The ACF text also uses rhetorical questions to involve the reader—four of them in Text 3.1:

> What men and women would we be if we did not care for the lives and . . .?

> What will killing 3 million kangaroos a year do for us as human beings?

> What sort of Australians can shrug off that kind of brutality?

> And what are the implications for the rest of nature, for the bush, . . .?

None of these is a genuine question. The answers are obvious—only cruel uncaring men and women could enjoy the sufferings of fellow creatures; only thoughtless Australians could shrug off the brutality, and so on. But the reader does have to fill in some set of answers to interpret the meaning of the text. And this means the reader is participating with the writer in making the points the editorial is trying to get across. The CWF text attempts this only once:

> Is this because seals are a national resource, or has the media been naively manipulated by opponents of the seal hunt?

This question is in fact difficult to answer; I personally have problems figuring out what it means or what the connection is between its two parts. Because of this it is less than effective in Text 3.2.

Note that Text 3.2 starts off with a real question, but that this is not a question to the reader. Rather, it is constructed as a question that might be lingering in the minds of readers which puts the CWF into an information-giving role. In this sense it is less involving than the suggestions and rhetorical questions used in the ACF text.

Overall then these structures help establish the ACF writer—reader relationship as a more participatory interactive one—of equal to equal. The CWF text's writer—reader relation is an impersonal one—that of expert passing on information to the uninformed.

Expressing attitudes

What about the expression of attitude? In Chapter 2, we noted that, in general, expository writing is less expressive than speaking, although Hortatory Exposition tends to be more expressive than Analytical. And this turns out to be the case in Texts 3.1 and 3.2. The ACF text does attempt to stir the reader. Reference to the killing of kangaroos is often strongly attitudinal:

> the <u>massive</u> level of killing
> <u>trusting</u> targets
> whose lives will be <u>obliterated</u>, often painfully
> <u>sufferings</u> of our fellow creatures

the <u>imposed</u> death of millions
that kind of <u>brutality</u>
our <u>prime</u> wildlife is killed on this scale

Reference to the Right protagonists the ACF is struggling against is also attitudinally marked:

our rather <u>smug</u> government biologists
the <u>pathetic</u> lack of supervisory staff

The CWF text is of course less expressive. But when it comes to the question of truth and fiction, it does make use of attitudinal lexis:

<u>unequivocally</u> yes
<u>false</u> and <u>misleading</u>
<u>sensational</u> news item
<u>naively</u> manipulated

In short then, the ACF text is more expressive than the CWF one; and the two texts are expressive about different things. The ACF text focuses attitudinal expressions on the killing of kangaroos; the CWF text focuses its emotive language on what it considers to be misleading statements by the Left protagonists and antagonists. This is yet another dimension on which we can see that the ACF text is more oriented to people and their feelings than the CWF text, which is concerned with the facts of the matter.

Intensification

Closely related to the question of attitude is the way in which Texts 3.1 and 3.2 emphasise certain points. The major device used in Text 3.1 is that of grammatical parallelism. The last six sentences of Text 3.1 make extensive use of this device. Firstly, three rhetorical questions are posed, with the third longer than the other two:

What will killing 3 million kangaroos a year do for us as human beings?

What sort of Australians can shrug off that kind of brutality?

And what are the implications for the rest of nature, for the bush, for the land, for other animals, for our fellow human beings, when our prime wildlife is killed on this scale?

The last of these of course contains no less than five parallel prepositional phrases beginning with *for*. Then a statement is put forward, followed by two minor clauses which replay the structure of the nominal group *our own perception of ourselves as Australians* (the first part of the structure of that group in fact); the second of these minor clauses is shorter than the first, giving a wavelike movement from the first rhetorical question through to the last minor clause:

In the end we are talking about our own perception of ourselves as Australians.

Our nationhood, our identity, our national pride and self-respect.

Our humanity.

This rhetorical device is a well-known feature of spoken Hortatory Exposition—it reminds us of the language of debates, political speeches, sermons, and the like. This is another way in which written Hortatory Exposition is more like spoken language than Analytical Exposition.

The main device used for intensification in Text 3.2 is bold face type. This is used to emphasise the thesis of the text: that the clubbing of seals is humane; and to highlight the definition of a humane death used in the argument. So the resources of written rather than spoken language are being used for emphasis when this is required. As we would expect, the CWF text makes less use of intensification than the ACF text. Expressive and emphatic language is felt to be inappropriately emotional for Analytical Exposition in our culture. Note that the CWF text is quite explicit about the fact that emotion should not be used when discussing the ecological issue at stake:

> Statements to that effect are false and misleading, designed to generate an <u>emotional</u> response to an otherwise normal operation.

Expressions of certainty and necessity

Finally, let's take a brief look at the way in which Texts 3.1 and 3.2 express how sure they are about what they are saying and what kind of obligations they see as relevant to the discussion. Firstly, certainty.

As we might expect, given its strong orientation to sorting out facts from fiction, the CWF text is more overtly categorical than the ACF text. This it accomplishes mainly through explicitly negative and positive statements:

> The answer to that question is <u>unequivocally</u> **Yes**.
>
> There is no <u>aesthetically</u> <u>pleasant way</u>. . .
>
> there is <u>no way it can be made a pretty sight</u>.
>
> It is however, <u>neither cruel nor a massacre</u>.
>
> Statements to that effect are <u>false and misleading</u>.
>
> There is <u>little doubt</u> that. . .

While the ACF text presents its case strongly—there is little hedging or tentative language—it does not make use of as many categorical expressions of this kind as the CWF text.

As far as necessity is concerned, it is worth noting that the CWF text expresses necessity twice in an impersonal way:

> However, it is <u>necessary</u> to recognise that . . . (cf. <u>You must</u> recognise that . . .)
>
> It is <u>necessary</u> to question how . . . (cf. <u>We must</u> question how . . .)

In Text 3.2 then the adjective *necessary* is used alongside the impersonal subject *it* to realise necessity. This way of coding necessity is typical of Analytical Exposition. By comparing it with the typical spoken alternatives given in brackets above, which make use of a personal pronoun subject and a modal verb, we can see why this is the case. The spoken version makes explicit whether the writer or the reader is the one who must act; and the necessity becomes debatable (e.g. *We must question . . .—Must you?—Yes, we must.*) The impersonal way of realising necessity is felt to be more objective, and so is characteristic of Analytical Exposition.

Protagonists changing the world

In the section 'Ideology and genre', we looked at the way in which issues arise as protagonists and antagonists argue about the way in which power is shared. A large number of genres are of course involved in these debates. And in the section 'Differences between the Hortatory and Analytical texts' we looked at an example of the way in which Hortatory and Analytical Expositions are used by protagonists to challenge and maintain the status quo.

See pp. 36–40.

By looking at Texts 3.1 and 3.2 in detail we saw why Right protagonists favour Analytical Exposition. They like to appear rational and present the way power is shared at a given time as simply a fact of life. Analytical Exposition is a good way of presenting the status quo as a kind of immutable given, which people can't really do much about and where feelings have no place. Left protagonists on the other hand prefer Hortatory Exposition. This form of factual writing is more suitable for stirring readers' emotions and persuading them to challenge the way things are. It is more active and holds out the possibility of change, brought about by people, because of what they think **and** feel.

See pp. 41–7.

Analytical Exposition tends to support the status quo, while Hortatory Exposition tends to challenge it.

Before summing up this part of the book and turning to the question of latent ideology in Chapter 4, we need to look again at Texts 3.1 and 3.2, this time from the point of view of the ideology of the protagonists involved. One thing we need to take into account is that the Left and Right protagonists are aware of each other's texts, and do try to undermine the language used by their opponents. We can see three of the ways in which they do this in Texts 3.1 and 3.2.

First of all they make fun of terms used by the other side. Sometimes scare quotes are used to make explicit the fact that these terms are being borrowed from the opposition. Thus in the ACF text we find *species survival*, *harvests*, *quotas*, and *management* all used in contexts which mock the terminology of the Right protagonists in ecological debates. Similarly the CWF text explicitly points out that the terms *cruel* and *massacre* are terms which appeal to emotion, not reason.

Secondly, not just terms, but whole phrases may be lifted from the language of the opposing protagonist. Thus the ACF text mocks their opponents' way of speaking with both *We may not be able to cost out our feeling* and *that narrower view that measures survival in species*. Similarly the question which heads the CWF text, *Is the clubbing of seals humane?*, is taken from one of the charges of the Left protagonists that it is not humane at all.

Finally, the enemy may be explicitly mentioned, often in a derogatory way. The ACF text refers to the Right protagonists as *our rather smug government biologists*. Later in the editorial they refer to *authorities with the word wildlife in their name* (as the CWF of course does). The CWF text is more restrained. But the media is singled out in Text

3.2, and described as having *naively permitted itself to be manipulated by opponents of the hunt.*

So the texts of the Left and Right protagonists as issues arise are clearly pitted against each other; many of the linguistic choices made in such texts can only be understood in the context of debate over ideological issues.

The second point we need to look at before moving on to Chapter 4 has to do with the way in which each side argues its case. Here we are not so much concerned with point scoring and refutation as with the general thrust of the rationale on each side. This is where the metaphors discussed in Chapter 2 come in. The main technique that is used is to change the nature of the issue being debated in such a way that it is clear what should be done. In ecological debates, this is done by treating the river, plant, or animal in question in different ways.

Recalling the opposition profile in Figure 3.5, exploiters (the Right antagonists) try to shift the debate from one about the environment to one about business. Seals and kangaroos are treated as commercial products, rather than wild animals. Users (the Right protagonists) attempt to treat the issue as a question about how to skilfully use renewable resources. They treat seals and kangaroos like trees or fish. Observers (the Left protagonists) try to shift the issue into the field of ecology. For them seals and kangaroos are threatened species. Preservers (the Left antagonists) approach the question as a criminal one. They view seals and kangaroos as people; to kill them is a kind of murder. These positions are summed up in Figure 3.8.

Figure 3.8 Shifting the debate in ecological issues

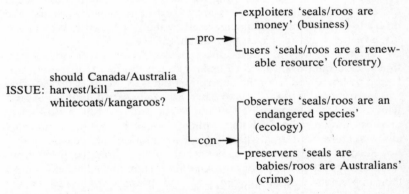

The CWF text we examined was very clear about treating seals as a renewable resource, and refers to seal taking as the *whitecoat harvest.* As well, it explicitly refers to this harvest as a *slaughtering operation* not unlike those carried out in approved government abattoirs on domestic animals. Implicitly, the argument is as follows: No one worries about harvesting wheat or eating meat, so why should they worry about killing seals? An attempt is made to change the issue from one about which people are uncertain, to one about which they have no doubts. Again, this shift significantly affects a large number of choices in the text which need to be taken into account. The metaphor is implicit—

the CWF does not argue that seals are like wheat. But the grammar and lexis make this message very clear.

Text 3.1, the ACF text, starts off with the argument that kangaroos are an endangered species. This argument is developed extensively in those sections of the editiorial not included here. But most of Text 3.1 itself is in fact reminiscent of the arguing used by the Left antagonists rather than protagonists. As far as possible, kangaroos are identified as Australians:

> that web of life embracing the human species as well as the easy, trusting targets in the night spotlights.

> 3 million other living creatures whose lives will be obliterated . . .

> the lives and sufferings of our fellow creatures . . .

> our fellow-creatures

> our prime wildlife

The article as a whole concludes by referring to kangaroos as *our national symbol*:

> It will be an index of our civilisation when we stop the killing on such a scale, take a price off the head of our national symbol and fund thorough programmes to conserve our wildlife.

The proposal here is very clear. Kangaroos may not quite be people, but they are the next best thing—our national symbol—and we have no more right to treat them as animals to be hunted down and shot than we do to murder people. The debate is shifted to the criminal arena. The rationale of the metaphor here is: We don't murder our fellow human beings, so we shouldn't murder kangaroos.

Spelled out as we have done here, both arguments are silly. Seals are not trees or wheat or swine. Kangaroos aren't people. But both texts take reasoning of this kind and use it somewhat perversely to shift the debate in their favour. In fact, reasoning of this kind has a powerful effect on the success of expository texts in convincing readers one way or the other and its importance cannot be underestimated.

Is factual writing 'factual'?

There is a naive view in our culture that it is possible to distinguish form from content, and that factual writing deals with content and can be judged simply in terms of how truthful or close to the facts it is. Hopefully we have now looked closely enough at factual writing that you can see just how naive this view is. There are no 'facts' out there against which we can measure the truthfulness or accuracy of a text. Facts are created by language as we speak or write. Factual writing is an interpretation of the world, not its reflection. It's not a question of how good our mirror is. Much more important is whether or not we interpret the world as others in our culture do; and if we see things differently, whether we can write effectively enough to convince them that we are not mad. Because of this, factual writing requires all the creativity and imagination we can muster if it is to succeed. It is highly metaphorical. It may be contentious. And it matters in a way that stories do not. People who have not mastered expository writing cannot really change the world; nor can they work effectively to keep it from changing in ways they don't like. They may not even be able to understand the language of the protagonists who we charge with these responsibilities. Exposition counts, even if it has nothing to do with truth.

In the last chapter of this book we are going to look at a culture in which infants' and primary schools make very little use of factual writing of any kind. This has very serious consequences for the lives of the children treated in this way and we will attempt to analyse the ideology of a culture that treats children like this. In a sense we will be turning from ideology in crisis, which has been the focus of Chapter 3, to latent ideology—the system of beliefs that determines people's shares in power without their realising it. Control of written genres is very much tied up with the distribution of power in all literate cultures.

Expository writing is important to changing the world.

50

Chapter 4

The way things are: children writing in infants' and primary school

In 1983 Joan Rothery and I looked closely at the kinds of writing undertaken by infants' and primary school children in one suburban school in the Sydney region. The school was in its second year of 'process' writing, inspired by the work of Graves (1983) and his Australian protagonists, Walshe (1981) and Turbill (1982). One thing we were interested in was the kind of writing the children did—which genres they wrote. We have now analysed about two-thirds of the writing collected with this question in mind (about 1500 texts). In this chapter we will look at some of our findings and try to comment on why schools concentrate on a few school genres at the expense of writing of other kinds.

Writing and power

As cultures develop writing systems and so become literate, writing and ideology interact from the start in predictable ways. For one thing, not everyone will learn to write. This is true of even the most technologically advanced Western cultures. Naturally it is the powerful that learn to write first, and this in itself increases their power. In time, a large number of written genres arise which are not found in speaking: newspaper articles, reports, editorials, etc.; textbooks of various types; kinds of institutional records; laws and legislation; and so on. As the functions of writing and speaking diverge, those who are literate become even more powerful, at the expense of those who are not.

Alongside this an important change takes place in people's attitudes to language. Whereas once speaking was good enough for everyone, and the most prestigious users of language were great orators, writing gradually becomes more important than speaking. The most prestigious users of language become writers, not speakers. And written language is prized above speech. This attitude in itself further increases the power of literate people. Written language is taken as the model for all language use; and the language of people who cannot read and write is downgraded. It even becomes important on public occasions to talk as if one was writing, as noted in Chapter 2. Talking like a book

Writing has become the prestige language form, while speech is undervalued.

51

is highly valued, and writing starts to have a big influence on the way in which people speak, especially powerful public figures.

These developments lead to a culture in which pedantry and snobbery conspire to blatantly discriminate against the language of large sections of the community. For one thing, different social classes tend to speak different dialects. And writing models itself on the dialect of the ruling class. So if you speak a dialect of English which says 'I seen it' instead of 'I saw it', your speech will be downgraded (note how the words *ignorant*, *lazy*, *uneducated*, *incorrect*, etc. are used by pedants to describe dialectal differences of this kind). Another factor involved here is that languages change. No one talks now the way Chaucer or Shakespeare did. But because people take writing as their model of what language is like, most of these changes are frowned upon when they first arise. People try to keep these changes out of writing as long as possible, in an effort to keep the language from 'degenerating'. English, for example, lost its case marking systems in the Middle Ages; but there are still pedants who insist on distinguishing *who* from *whom* in writing—needless to say, nobody makes this distinction in speaking (unless they are talking like a book!). Again, these prescriptive grammarians do their best to make literate people aware of the ways in which the spoken language is evolving by proscribing these changes in writing. People who do not have access to the older written forms then find their language criticised because they are moving with the times. Finally, pedants often introduce grammatical rules from foreign languages into another language. In English, pedants have often made use of Latin grammar in this way (the rule against splitting infinitives is a good example). Again, people who are not fully socialised into writing of this kind find themselves at a disadvantage.

A large part of linguists' objections to the use made of grammar in schools in fact stems from the way it is used to derogate and proscribe the language of large sections of the community. Unfortunately this has probably contributed to the erosion of grammar teaching of any kind in schools, which is certainly not what linguists had in mind. Even the debased version of scholarly traditional grammar which came to be used in schools in the 19th century is better than no grammar at all, if only for the reason that it makes useful grammars easier to learn. To see the difference between scholarly traditional grammar and school grammar, compare the Quirk et al. (1972) *Grammar of Contemporary English* with any school grammar you have to hand. In a sense school grammars are about prejudice rather than language structure.

The pedantry and snobbery which develops alongside literacy is politically relevant in many ways. Recently, for example, my own university, the elite and prestigious University of Sydney, decided that applicants had to include English in the marks they used to compete for places in all faculties. The reasons for this had to do with an unsubstantiated concern with falling literacy standards in the university. I tried to point out to the people concerned that there was no real evidence that standards were falling (hysterical outbursts about falling literacy standards occur every few years in our culture and simply reflect the use of spoken forms in contexts where pedants deem them inappropriate) and that in any case English departments in secondary schools do not teach the kinds of reading and writing skills the university is looking for. Ten years of narrative/expressive writing and two years of literary criticism in no way prepare one for the writing demands of the diverse faculties in universities. As usual, the pedants won the day. It was decided that English marks should be included—with the result that large numbers of working-class, migrant, Aboriginal, and foreign students will be discriminated against in the selection procedures. This will make the university even more elitist than before at a time when the government in Canberra is encouraging universities to open up admissions to students from less privileged sections of the community. This is just one example of the way in which the ruling class (in the sense of Connell et al. 1982) in our culture exploits ignorance and prejudice about language to become even more powerful.

Learning what to write

Most people learn to read and write in school. We should be careful, however, about the way in which we use these terms in this context. We must be cautious because when we use the verbs *reading* and *writing* intransitively, we are obscuring an important distinction. Suppose, for example, someone is talking, say in a courtroom, and someone is writing down what they say as a legal record. Now clearly this process is writing; but it is writing of a special kind—the clerk is writing down what someone is saying. Technically we should refer to this process as TRAN- SCRIPTION, to make it clear that we are talking about writing down speech. This is in fact the way in which most people think of writing. They think of learning to write as learning to write down what we would otherwise say.

The problem with this intransitive view of writing is that it doesn't take into account the vast differences between speaking and writing. Writing in fact involves more than transcription. Learning to write involves learning new genres and new ways of using grammar as well. If we look at writing transitively we must always ask: write **what?** The failure to ask this queston lies at the heart of most of the problems educational theorists are causing for children as far as teaching writing is concerned.

Learning to write always involves learning to write different genres and new ways of using grammar.

So let's start asking the question. What do children write in infants' and primary school?

Types of writing in infants' and primary school

So far in our analysis Joan Rothery and I have looked at about 1500 texts from Years 1–6 from this point of view. We collected all the writing done by their classes once a term. So our sample is fairly representative of what is going on. Of the 1500 texts considered so far, only 228 (15 per cent) were factual writing. We found 189 Reports (13 per cent), 31 Procedures (2 per cent), and 8 Explanations and Expositions (0.5 per cent). Most of the other 1272 texts were writing of the narrative/expressive kind.

The six writers we focused on in each grade were classified as good, average, and poor writers by their teachers. When we take this into account, we find that up to Year 6, most of the factual writing is accomplished by the good writers; and in Year 6, it is the good and average writers who write most of the Reports, Procedures, and Explanations and Expositions. This means overall that average writers are starting factual writing very late and that poor writers are doing almost no factual writing at all. It is very clear from these results that the writing skills used by the ruling class are not considered very important for young children; and that these skills are being passed on selectively to just a few bright children. In order to understand why this is happening we need to look closely at the ideology of the culture which sponsors education of this kind. In particular we need to look at that culture's attitude to children. It is here that we need to begin looking at latent ideology.

Children

Latent ideology is hard to unpack. Not only is it unconscious, like most of the rest of the meaning systems in which we live, but it seems to be almost purposely buried. Just talking about it makes most people uncomfortable. The message that often comes across is that what you are saying is wrong, and even if you're right, they'd rather simply not know about it. With this warning in mind, let's begin. We'll start with a list, in no particular order, of nine attitudes which our culture for the most part adopts towards children. All have a fascinating intellectual history, which regrettably your author has neither the time nor the competence to adequately describe here (see Ariès 1973 for a more scholarly approach to some of these ideas). Each of these attitudes is relevant to the kinds of writing children do and the ways in which writing is not taught:

1. Children are individuals.
2. Children are spontaneous learners.
3. Children are cognitively immature.
4. Children are creative.
5. Children are innocent.
6. Children are egocentric.
7. Children are imaginative.
8. Children are ignorant.
9. Children are irresponsible.

Children are individuals

The idea here, and it is a deeply rooted one in Western culture, is that children, like everyone else, are first and foremost individuals. Everyone has their own identity, which needs to be fostered. This seems to be part of the reason why schools are reluctant to teach children the conventions of writing in different genres and to provide models for them to use. The fear is that conventions and models will tend to make children all write the same. They would then lose their individuality.

Children are spontaneous learners

Here the idea seems to be that children learn language spontaneously. There is no need to instruct them directly about written genres. All that is needed is for the teacher to produce a rich and stimulating language environment. In such an environment the child's spontaneous learning abilities will flourish and she will acquire whatever language is necessary to write well.

Children are cognitively immature

Under the influence of folk-psychology, many teachers believe that children move through stages of cognitive development and that these stages are relevant to the kinds of writing children do. Certain types of writing, factual writing in particular, are felt to be beyond children of certain ages. Narrative/expressive writing is felt to be simpler, and more appropriate in infants' and primary school.

Children are creative

Here we encounter the belief that all children are potential poets and artists, and that society tends to crush the natural creativity we all once possessed. Narrative is felt to offer more opportunities for creativity than factual writing. Factual writing seems to be associated with the burdens of society that destroy the creative spark.

Children are innocent

Most adults look back on' childhood nostalgically as a time of play, free from the responsibilities of adult life. Many feel that children need to be protected from adult burdens as long as possible so that they can enjoy being a child. Again, factual writing is seen as an incursion of the adult world into the child's state of grace.

Children are egocentric

Folk-psychology is again relevant here, as with the discussion of cognitive immaturity above. Many people believe that children have trouble taking other people's points of view into account and are much more interested in their own world of experience. This is one reason why so much Recount writing takes place. Teachers leave it up to the child to select their own topics and children then tend to write about what they have been doing. Factual writing usually involves exploring other people's experiences as well and children are not thought to be interested in these or capable of investigating them.

Children are imaginative

Many people think that children have trouble distinguishing between fantasy and reality and that they really prefer to live in a world of dreams or play. Narrative provides lots of opportunities for imaginative writing and so provides more scope for a child's imagination. Children are felt to be more interested in make-believe than in exploring the reality they are growing up into.

Children are ignorant

Children are considered young and not very well informed about the world. The only thing they really know about is their own experience and this is what they should write about. Again, this leads to Recount writing. Children are not expected to know enough about the world to engage in much writing of a factual kind.

Children are irresponsible

There is also a view that unless adults keep the lid on, children might erupt into *Lord of the Flies* style anarchy. This seems to be reflected in bans some teachers place on the blood and guts style of narrative that interests many young boys. Writing of this kind is seen as reflecting tendencies which need to be checked.

What are children really like?

From the point of view of linguistics, each of these attitudes towards children can be strongly challenged. Let me put the case provocatively, and leave the resolution of these issues to you.

Would you prefer to write Hortatory or Analytical Expositions when tackling these issues?

1. Children are social beings who learn language through interactions with other people in an environment which provides highly structured models of the way in which people talk and use language.

2. Children first learn language from the models presented by parents and peers; once they learn to talk they begin to use language to learn; language can be used to learn about language just as well as it can be used to learn about mathematics or science or whatever; there is no reason why genres could not be taught.

3. Without teachers' encouragement, children take up factual writing in infants school; there are no cognitive reasons why factual writing could not begin much earlier than it does.

4. Children are not creative in the same way that poets and artists are **until** they have mastered the genres in which they are writing; children's mistakes when learning a genre are often misunderstood as creative; they are, however, not systematically motivated patterns as with mature artists.

5. Being a child is not the carefree happy time adults think it is; children have problems, like everybody else; they long to grow up and do what adults do; they dislike being told they can't.

6. Many children are interested in other people's experience. They do read for information, not just for fun. Boys in particular at certain ages often become extremely interested in the nature of things, setting themselves up as experts on trains, animals, space, warfare, etc.

7. Children have no more difficulty than adults in distinguishing fantasy from reality. Of course, like adults, they enjoy fantasy. But they are not confused—unless adults explicitly set out to make them so with stories of Santa Claus, the tooth fairy, storks, and the like.

8. Children of course know less than adults; but they love to learn. If they are taught the skills needed to do research, they will use them.

There is no need to restrict them to writing about their own experience.

9. Children appear irresponsible mainly because adults tend to assume responsibility for them all the time; in many cultures young children participate much more fully in adult tasks—of course they are young and make mistakes, but if they were given more responsibility in our culture, they'd become more responsible.

The main point of looking at children in this way is to point out that children are the least powerful group of people in our community. And the kinds of writing schools encourage them to do reflects this powerlessness. The Analytical Exposition they could use to explore and interpret their world is denied them as long as possible. One gets the feeling that if it wasn't for exams, it might be denied them altogether. And the Hortatory Exposition children might use to challenge their world, including the share of power they have in it, is never really developed, even in secondary school. Children's writing is the writing of the powerless. Unconsciously, the education system has developed a way of not teaching children to write that helps keep them as powerless as possible. Whatever people's intentions, this is the way in which writing and power are related in our schools.

> Children are the least powerful group in our community.

Sexism

As noted in Chapter 1, in our work we also noticed a number of differences in the kinds of writing done by boys and girls. These differences have to do with what children wrote as well as the genres they chose to write; and they got bigger as the children progressed through infants' and primary school. As Poynton notes in the book *Language and Gender* (1989), girls write about family, dress, appearance, pets, and romance (the **nurture** of things as I have it) and fantasy worlds inhabited by fairies, witches, and characters from the stories they read. Boys, on the other hand, write about zoos, radios, sport, trains, and war (the **nature** of things) and adventures involving their own BMX bikes, science fiction, monster stories, crime, and so on. As far as genre is concerned, boys are more likely than girls to write Reports without being asked; they make more use of humour, spoofing genres, and annotating texts with cartoons; and their narratives often seem more influenced by the media than by reading—crisis piles up upon crisis in a kind of serialised narrative format reminiscent of an Indiana Jones spectacular. Boys are admired by teachers and peers alike for their humour; but teachers generally prefer narratives to Reports, and Enid Blyton narratives to serials—as noted above boys may even find their serialised or excessively violent narration banned for days and weeks at a time. It sometimes looks as if they are being discriminated against in a sexist way by women teachers. But in the long run they will more than benefit from the encouragement girls receive in narrative writing and their distinctive interest in the nature rather than the nurture of things. (For a discussion of related gendering of writing in Britain, see White, 1986).

Now again, we need to ask what kind of culture it is that unconsciously promotes sex differences in writing such as these. At least five distinct factors appear to contribute to the latent ideology underlying such differences:

1. Boys are irreverent/girls conform.
2. Boys watch TV/girls read.
3. Boys have adventures/girls play house.
4. Boys explore the nature/girls the nurture, of things.
5. Boys perform in public/girls seek quiet praise.

Boys are irreverent/girls conform

First of all, it is boys, not girls, who buck the system. In general they are harder to control and more likely to resist authority (these differences are of course magnified in mixed sex schools). Some of the topics they choose to write about, especially the blood and guts narration, seem designed to shock. And through humour they deal irreverently with many of the conventions society is passing on to them. Girls are more accepting, sensitive to what infants' and primary school teachers subconsciously prize, and they write to please.

Boys watch TV/girls read

Middle-class girls seem to be more influenced by reading than by TV in their writing. Their narratives model themselves on children's literature. We are not sure whether girls actually read more than boys. But whatever the case it is not reading, but TV, video, and movies that seem to influence boys' narrative. It may also be that boys read more non-fictional material, which provides them with information on which to base the Reports that are not assigned to them by teachers as part of a social science theme.

Some of these issues are examined in Steedman (1983).

Boys have adventures/girls play house

The different kinds of play in which boys and girls engage appear as well to be responsible for the topics they write about. Boys tend to play outside in wolf-packs, having make-believe and real adventures on their BMX bikes. Girls play in groups of two or three inside or around the house. Boys often include several of their mates in adventure stories; if girls appear, they do so as enemies. Girls almost never include boys in their stories. And sport of course figures much more in the writing of boys than girls; it is treated as another form of adventure by them.

Boys explore the nature/girls the nurture, of things

As noted above, some boys, in primary school, become deeply interested in one or another topic: trains, war, space, science, etc. And as experts they may produce large numbers of Reports based on the information they have mastered. Girls, on the other hand, seem more involved in the nurture of things. Stories based on family conflict, divorce for example, will almost certainly be written by girls, as opposed to boys. Boys in other words take an interest in knowledge about the world; girls, in how people relate. And this affects both what they write about and the genres they choose.

Boys perform publicly/girls seek quiet praise

Boys are more likely than girls to try to be the centre of attention in a class. Through blood and guts narration they are singled out and reprimanded by their teacher. Similarly, their serialised narratives may be banned. On the positive side, their cartoons and spoofs may bring them the admiration of all concerned. Successful girls' narrative, reflective and caring as it often is, tends to draw a less public response from the teacher—an encouraging written comment or a word of quiet praise. Boys draw public attention to themselves, often as rebels, in their writing as in other ways; girls seek out a quieter and less public kind of success.

For anyone interested in feminism, these traits will be all too familiar (again, see Poynton 1989). One scarcely needs to show how arbitrary and discriminatory such differences between boys and girls are. From the point of view of this book the important thing to note is that boys are more interested in information and factual writing than girls; and that girls are being encouraged in their narrative writing while boys are not. So even in infants' and primary school boys are being unconsciously turned towards the kinds of writing that are powerful in our culture. Girls are being depowered from the very first stages of literacy. It is natural that the power invoked in certain types of writing by the ruling class would be passed on to boys and girls in this way. Sexism typically mirrors class power in the Western world.

Capitalism

This brings us to the final layer of ideological interpretation to be covered here—capitalism. In order to fully understand the childist and sexist ideologies at work in schools, it is important to understand the function of education systems in Western capitalist societies and also the kind of families that capitalism has produced.

Nuclear families: children as entertaining pets

We often watch friends treating their pets like children. The question I would like to put here is whether or not we can turn this formulation around: do parents in our culture also treat children as pets? Our answer depends on our interpretation of the family.

As Ariès (1973) points out, the large extended family of the Middle Ages has gradually been replaced in modern society with the small, independent nuclear family consisting of two adults and a small number of children; this change has perhaps been most dramatic over the last two generations. Alongside the emergence of the nuclear family, the differences between children and adults and the amount of time children have to spend in childhood have been continually increased, especially recently. Whereas once children participated with their parents in adult work and play at a very young age, in our society children remain in school well into their teens or even later, are politically deprived in all ways until their late teens (well after sexual maturity), and are treated differently from adults in almost every way. The main function of children in modern families appears to be simply that of entertaining adults. Children are kept as childlike as possible for as long as possible.

Children in our culture remain 'childlike' for a long time.

59

See pp. 54–7.

In this way the pleasure adults in Western society get from watching kids grow up is extended by many years. The childist attitudes involved in this process have already been discussed above in the section 'Children'. The economic reasons for the growth of nuclear families have been the subject of a great deal of intellectual inquiry and cannot be pursued here. Suffice it to say that capitalism changed the nature of families and of children's place in these families. This has led to discrimination against children of an unparalleled kind. The depowering types of writing undertaken by children until senior secondary school reflect this extension of childhood and differentiation of children from adults.

Education: controlling children

In capitalist countries the major function of education is not to train children for jobs, but to control a large sector of the community for which capitalism cannot provide work. At present in Australia, for example, greater unemployment has led to children staying longer in school. This is not because schools have changed and are all of a sudden preparing children for work better than before. It is simply that children have no attractive alternative. There is no work, so they remain at school. Because education is not directly involved in preparing children for employment and because Western society is determined to keep children childlike as long as possible, the major function of education becomes that of controlling children and socialising them as relatively passive receptors of the status quo—all this of course needs to be done as economically as possible. For this reason the kinds of writing that would allow children to understand and challenge the system in which they live are withheld until the last possible minute when in a hysterical two-year burst of preparation for final examinations they are used as a kind of threatening weapon with which to further suppress young adults. The need to learn to write the Analytical Exposition upon which their future depends in just two years at the end of secondary school is a powerful tool for controlling children at an age when they are least likely to accept the childlike status which society has extended even further since the Second World War.

Education: keeping children off the dole

This point is closely related to the preceding one, but has a slightly different emphasis. Education is concerned with controlling children and withholding powerful writing until the last possible moment in order to do so. But as well, education ignores almost completely the kinds of writing that would enable children to enter the workforce. I have spent a number of years working as a consultant for the CSIRO in Canberra, looking at the kinds of writing undertaken there in order to design a writing course for new administrative recruits. It is very clear from this short visit that the several types of bureaucratic writing needed there were very different from the essays and narratives written by the recruits in high school and university. Bureaucratese, for all its strengths and failings, is a type of writing the recruits will have to learn on the job.

60

If schools did train children for jobs, and taught them the skills, including the writing skills they needed, then children would be ready to work years before graduation. Since the function of education is in fact to keep children from competing for jobs, the kinds of writing they could use later are unconsciously suppressed.

Education: reproducing social difference

One of the most important functions of education is to reproduce the social order existing in our community. Sex roles and the differences between ruling and working classes must be passed on. There are many ways in which this is achieved, but one of the most effective is to make as unclear as possible what exactly it is that has to be learned to succeed. If children received explicit instruction in writing, for example, including models and direct teaching making use of knowledge about language, many more children would learn to write effectively than at present. And success in education depends on writing. But at present, writing is not taught. Bright middle-class children learn by osmosis what has to be learned. Working-class, migrant, or Aboriginal children, whose homes do not provide them with models of writing, and who don't have the coding orientation (in Bernstein's sense) to read between the lines and see what is implicitly demanded, do not learn to write effectively.

Some of these issues are explored in Bernstein (1971, 1973, 1975).

Ironically, almost every liberal initiative in education since the Second World War as far as language in education is concerned has had the effect of making what has to be learned less and less visible. Process writing (Graves 1983) is the latest of these initiatives. With its stress on ownership and voice, its preoccupation with children selecting their own topics, its reluctance to intervene positively and constructively during conferencing, and its complete mystification of what has to be learned for children to produce effective written products, it is currently promoting a situation in which only the brightest middle-class children can possibly learn what is needed. Conferencing is used not to teach but to obscure. This kind of refusal to teach helps reinforce the success of ruling-class children in education; through an insidious benevolence other children are supportively encouraged to fail. Liberalism as it is currently practised in these forms is the major enemy of children, women, working-class kids, migrants, and Aboriginal children in Australian education.

What is to be done?

I will make this section very short. If these discriminatory practices are to be erased, and the latent ideology underlying them challenged, then children need to be taught the writing of power as early as possible. The sooner they control factual writing of different kinds, the sooner they will be able to understand and challenge the world in which we live. And they need to be taught to write; only a few of them can learn it on their own.

Epilogue

As you are no doubt well aware, I have written Chapter 4 in a provocative way. In a sense I have tried to function as a Left antagonist, though I have generally used Analytical Exposition rather than a bomb to stir up the issues with which I am concerned. My main aim has been to show that most of what we commonly think about factual writing is part of an ideological conspiracy that treats Exposition as work and narrative as play and discriminates against children and women by encouraging them to play instead of work for so many years. When factual writing is finally introduced seriously in secondary school, it is seen as a burden rather than as a powerful tool and the reasons given for doing it have to do with exams rather than discovery and social change. All this plays into the hands of the ruling class. It enhances their status and power and represses those who are already down.

The question is of course: is this what education should be about? Few people I think would answer yes to this question. But at the same time they would likely argue that most of what I am saying misses the point. They would point to the virtues of narrative and expressive writing of different kinds (which let me stress I am in no way denying), the evils of the outside world, and the problems of cognitive development. In reply let me suggest that people start asking a simple question: who gains power when people react in this way? And most of the time I think we will see that the people who argue against what I am saying are the ones who have most to lose if things were to change. As a general rule of thumb, people are much more likely to be saying what they mean when they stand to lose power through what they propose than if what they are saying promotes their own self-interest. We need to ask who the pedants are, who famous authors are, and who educational theorists are in all these debates. Looking at what people have to lose is a good way of uncovering the ideology behind what they are saying.

You could accuse me, like everyone else, of being after power. I want people to see that the way a linguist looks at language makes explicit what we implicitly know and explains why we do often act as we do. Conscious knowledge of language and the way it functions in social contexts then enables us to make choices, to exercise control. As long as we are ignorant of language, it and the ideological systems

Knowledge about language confers power.

62

it embraces control us. Learning about language means learning to choose. All choices are political. We don't write or talk just to pass the time away. To the extent that this book encourages you to make some choices that you hadn't thought about it will succeed. Knowledge is power. Meaning is choice. Please choose. With this lapse into Hortatory Exposition (when did I switch genres?), I will bring to a close this discussion of the nature and diverse functions of factual writing in our culture.

References

Ariès, P., *Centuries of Childhood: A Social History of Family Life*, Childhood in Society (Penguin, Harmondsworth, 1973).

Bernstein, B., *Class, Codes and Control*, vol. 1, *Theoretical Studies towards a Sociology of Language*, Primary Socialisation, Language and Education (Routledge & Kegan Paul, London, 1971).

Bernstein, B., *Class, Codes and Control*, vol. 2, *Applied Studies towards a Sociology of Language*, Primary Socialisation, Language and Education (Routledge & Kegan Paul, London, 1973).

Bernstein, B., *Class, Codes and Control*, vol. 3, *Towards a Theory of Educational Transmissions*, Primary Socialisation, Language and Education (Routledge & Kegan Paul, London, 1975).

Carr, J., Murphy, W., & Kindt, I., *In a Manner of Speaking: Teacher Notes and Suggested Activities* (Curriculum Services Branch, Department of Education, Brisbane, 1984).

Connell, R., Ashenden, D., Keffler, F., & Dowsett, G., *Making the Difference* (Allen & Unwin, Sydney, 1982).

Graves, D., *Writing: Teachers and Children at Work* (Heinemann, Exeter, 1983).

Halliday, M.A.K., *An Introduction to Functional Grammar* (Edward Arnold, London, 1985).

Halliday, M.A.K., *Spoken and Written Language* (Oxford University Press, Oxford, 1989).

Martin, J.R., 'Types of writing in infants and primary school', in L. Unsworth (ed.), *Reading, Writing, Spelling: Proceedings of the Fifth Macarthur Reading/Language Symposium* (Macarthur CAE, Sydney, pp. 34–55, 1984).

Martin, J.R., & Rothery, J., *Writing Report Project 1980*, Working Papers in Linguistics 1 (Department of Linguistics, University of Sydney, Sydney, 1980).

Martin, J.R., & Rothery, J., *Writing Report Project 1982*, Working Papers in Linguistics (Department of Linguistics, University of Sydney, Sydney, 1981).

Martin, J.R., & Rothery, J., 'What a functional approach to the writing task can show teachers about "good writing"', in B. Couture (ed.), *Functional Approaches to Writing: Research Perspectives*, Open Linguistic Series (Frances Pinter, London, 1986).

Poynton, C., *Language and Gender: Making the Difference* (Oxford University Press, Oxford, 1989).

Quirk, R., Greenbaum, S., Leech, G., & Svartvik, J., *A Grammar of Contemporary English* (Longman, London, 1972).

Steedman, C., *The Tidy House* (Virago, London, 1983).

Turbill, J., *No Better Way to Teach Writing* (Primary English Teaching Association, Sydney, 1982).

Walshe, R.D. (ed.), *Donald Graves in Australia* (Primary English Teaching Association, Sydney, 1981).

White, Janet, 'The writing on the wall: beginning or end of a girl's career?', *Women's Studies International Forum* 9.5.1986, pp. 561—574.

Further reading

The linguistic approach to children's writing development

Children Writing: Study Guide, ECT418 Language Studies (Deakin University, Geelong, Victoria, 1984).

Children Writing: Reader, ECT418 Language Studies (Deakin University, Geelong, Victoria, 1984).

Martin, J.R., & Peters, P, 'On the analysis of exposition', in R. Hasan (ed.), *Discourse on Discourse: Workshop Report from Macquarie Workshop on Discourse Analysis*, February 21–25, 1983 (Applied Linguistics Association of Australia, Melbourne, 1985).

Martin, J.R. & Rothery, J., 'What a functional approach to the writing task can show teachers about "good writing", in B. Couture (ed.), *Functional Approaches to Writing: Research Perspectives* (Frances Pinter, London 1986).

Christie, F., 'Some current issues in first language writing development', in H. Nicholas (ed.), *Current Issues in First and Second Language Development: Proceedings of the Working Party on Language Development* (Applied Linguistics Association of Australia, Melbourne, 1985).

Christie, F., 'Writing in schools: Generic structures as ways of meaning', in B. Couture (ed.), *Functional Approaches to Writing: Research Perspectives*, Open Linguistic Series, ed. R.P. Fawcett (Frances Pinter, London, 1985).

Collerson, John (ed.), *Writing for Life* (Primary English Teaching Association, Sydney, 1988).

The linguistic approach to children's writing development is introduced in the Deakin BEd course *Children Writing* (revised editions, titled *Writing in Schools* are currently in press); Martin & Peters, Christie, and Martin & Rothery provide relevant reading from this perspective. Frances Christie is interested in particular in the relationship of written genres to the spoken genres of schooling. Collerson brings together a number of papers focusing on genre-based approaches to literacy development in Australian primary schools..

Graves, D., *Writing: Teachers and Children at Work* (Heinemann, Exeter, 1983).

Walshe, R.D. (ed.), *Donald Graves in Australia* (Primary English Teaching Association, Sydney, 1981).

Turbill, J., *No Better Way to Teach Writing* (Primary English Teaching Association, Sydney, 1982).

Kress, G., *Learning to Write* (Routledge & Kegan Paul, London, 1982).

Thornton, G., *Teaching Writing: The Development of Written Language Skills*, Exploration in Language Study (Edward Arnold, London, 1980).

The process approach which is currently so fashionable in Australian schools can be studied in the Graves, Walshe, and Turbill volumes. Kress's *Learning to Write* and Thornton's *Teaching Writing* help balance this focus on process by taking written products into account.

Gray, B., 'Helping children to become language learners in the classroom', in P. Kidston & D. Patullo (eds.), *Reading and Writing: Implications for Teaching* (Meanjin Reading Council, Kelvin Grove, Queensland, 1984), pp. 141–166.

Walker, R., 'A language experience approach to language development', in P. Kidston & D. Patullo (eds.), *Reading and Writing: Implications for Teaching* (Meanjin Reading Council, Kelvin Grove, Queensland, 1984), pp. 135–40.

By far the best type of learning context as far as language development (including writing) is concerned has been developed by Dick Walker and Brian Gray at Traeger Park School in Alice Springs; Australian education tends to be dominated by approaches imported from Britain and America—this cultural cringe needs to be quickly overcome so that the quality of the teaching model described in the Gray and Walker papers can be better appreciated and inspire related projects elsewhere.

The linguistic model assumed in this book is a systemic functional one

Halliday, M.A.K., *An Introduction to Functional Grammar* (Edward Arnold, London, 1985).

Halliday, M.A.K. & Hasan, R., *Cohesion in English*, English Language Series 9 (Longman, London, 1976).

Halliday, M.A.K. & Hasan, R., *Language, Text, and Context* (Oxford University Press, Oxford, 1989).

Halliday, M.A.K., *Language as a Social Semiotic: The Social Interpretation of Language and Meaning* (Edward Arnold, London, 1978).

Gregory, M. & Carroll, S., *Language and Situation: Language Varieties and their Social Contexts* (Routledge & Kegan Paul, London, 1978).

Halliday's *Introduction to Functional Grammar* presents a comprehensive account of the way in which English grammar makes meaning; *Cohesion in English* adds on a textual perspective; and *Language, Text, and Context* relates both grammar and discourse to context. A more theoretical account of how it all fits together is given in Halliday's *Language as a Social Semiotic*; Gregory and Carroll is more accessible, but less detailed.

The approach to language and ideology taken here draws on the work of a number of linguists and sociologists

Whorf, B., *Language, Thought and Reality: Selected Readings*, ed. J.B. Carroll (MIT Press, Cambridge, Massachusetts, 1956).

Whorf's interpretation of language as constructing rather than reflecting reality is the crucial starting point.

Bernstein, B., *Class, Codes and Control*, vol.1 *Theoretical Studies towards a Sociology of Language*, Primary Socialisation, Language and Education) (Routledge & Kegan Paul, London, 1971).

Bernstein, B., *Class, Codes and Control*, vol. 2 *Applied Studies towards a Sociology of Language*, Primary Socialisation, Language and Education (Routledge & Kegan Paul, London, 1973).

Bernstein, B., *Class, Codes and Control*, vol. 3 *Towards a Theory of Educational Transmissions*, Primary Socialisation, Language and Education (Routledge & Kegan Paul, London, 1975).

Bernstein develops these ideas from the point of view of differences in outlook between different groups of speakers within a single language.

Kress, G. & Hodge, R., *Language as Ideology* (Routledge & Kegan Paul, London, 1979).

Fowler, R., Hodge, B., Kress, G. & Trew, T., *Language and Control* (Routledge & Kegan Paul, London, 1979).

These books tie these perspectives to the question of ideology.

Trudgill, P., *Sociolinguistics: An Introduction* (Penguin, Harmondsworth, 1974).

Stubbs, M., *Language, Schools & Classrooms* (Methuen, London, 1976).

Stubbs, M., *Language and Literacy* (Routledge & Kegan Paul, London, 1980).

Trudgill and Stubbs include good discussions of language variation which is relevant to the question of pedantry and prejudice discussed in the booklet.

Berger, P. L. & Luckmann, T., *The Social Construction of Reality: A Treatise in the Sociology of Knowledge* (Penguin, Harmondsworth, 1971).

Berger and Luckmann approach the question from sociology rather than linguistics, and show how the small talk of everyday life builds up the latent ideology in which we live.

Ariès, P., *Centuries of Childhood: A Social History of Family Life*, Childhood in Society (Penguin, Harmondsworth, 1973).

Ariès presents an invaluable study of the development of the child over the last few hundred years in our culture.

Connell, R., Ashenden, D., Keffler, F. & Dowsett, G., *Making the Difference* (Allen & Unwin, Sydney, 1982).

Connell et al. convincingly unveil the role of education in Australia as far as reproducing social difference is concerned.

Readings

Reading 1

Two varieties of writing: Report and Exposition

Joan Rothery

For the remainder of this paper I want to focus on two varieties of writing, Report and Exposition. Both play an important part in a student's secondary education. They are asked for in different subjects and in examinations. It is no exaggeration to say that a student's success in school will depend to a great extent on his mastery of these and some other varieties of writing.

The fact that Reports and Expositions are distinguished by different names indicates they are different. But how do they differ from each other? I would suggest to you that Reports and Expositions differ in as much as each has different goals and is structured differently to achieve these goals. Let me explain what I mean by describing the differences thus. The goal of expository writing is to persuade the reader of the truth or 'rightness' of a proposition; the goal of report writing is to describe the way things are. Each variety is structured to achieve its goal. The structure of Exposition can be represented thus:

Thesisˆ$Argument^n$ˆConclusion.

Thesis is the part of the text which presents the proposition to be argued. Argument is the writer's defence of or objections to the Thesis. The sign ˆ means that the element to the left of the sign precedes that to its right. The sign ^{n} indicates this part of the text can be repeated indefinitely. The structure of Report is General Classificationˆ$Description^n$. These structural descriptions represent the stages we go through to achieve our goals through language. In other words, types of writing are ways of achieving goals through language. It is for this reason we choose different varieties of writing.

Let us examine two texts which illustrate the text structures for report and expository writing. The first text, entitled 'The bat', is a Report.

Text 1   The bat
The bat is a nocturnal animal. It lives in the dark. There are long nosed bats and mouse eared bats also lettuce winged bats. Bats hunt at night. They sleep in the day and are very shy.

Source: J. Rothery, Writing to learn and learning to write. Paper delivered to an Inservice Study Day for the NSW Department of Education, 1985, pp. 9–26, 27, 28–9.

The first sentence in this text, *The bat is a nocturnal animal*, is a General Classification. The bat is classified as a type of animal. The remainder of the text is a description of types of bats and of their habits and characteristics. This part of the text is Description in the text structure. This text was written by a child in Year 2. So even at this early stage of schooling the writer has mastered the structure of report writing. It is likely that the child's writing has been influenced by his reading. When children read factual texts they are not only learning about what they read; they are also learning how factual texts are structured.

The second text is an expository essay.

Text 2   Are governments necessary? Give reasons for your answer

Yes, governments are necessary because it's the government which makes the rules of how our environment should be used, it's the government which makes up the councils, the banks, building societies, shopping centres, factories, or industries, etc.

The government also exports goods and imports goods and helps us in any way it can.

If governments didn't exist there would be thieves, burglars, and all sorts of criminals running around shooting everyone and there would be no one to stop them.

Governments also have smaller governments to look after the States, local areas, and suburbs.

This text was written by a much older student in Year 10 of the secondary school. The question set by the teacher made it clear that an exposition was required. There is a question to be answered: *are governments necessary?* By answering this question the writer formulates a Thesis. The other instruction tells the writer he must defend his thesis: *Give reasons for your answer*. The writer presents a Thesis in the opening sentence of his essay, *Yes, Governments are necessary*. He then proceeds to defend the Thesis with a number of arguments. This part of the essay is Argument in the text structure. There is a great deal we could say about the language of this essay. Most teachers would probably regard it as an immature piece of writing in many respects. But it is structured as exposition so the writer has accomplished something of importance. He is able to use the strategies for arguing that are considered effective in our society. We can thus be very positive in the comments we make about the essay. The basic text structure is there, to be worked on in constructive ways.

Text structure: a sociocultural phenomenon

There is a tendency to believe that only written texts, and only some written texts at that, are structured or ordered in the ways I have described for Report and Exposition. In fact, our language use in speech and writing is structured to achieve specific goals. We are not discussing a phenomenon specific to writing. We go through stages to achieve goals in making an appointment, consulting a doctor, buying different types of goods or going for a job interview. Consider, for example, buying and selling in our community. When we wish to purchase goods in a shop there are stages we go through to achieve this goal. Eija Ventola, a former student in the Linguistics Department at Sydney University, has described the structure of a buying and selling encounter in the following way:

Greeting
    Turn Allocation (selection of next customer: Who's next?)
    Service Bid (offer of service: Can I help you?)
    Service (statement of needs and their provision: Yes, I'm looking
       for . . .)
    Resolution (decision to buy or not to buy: Yes, I'll have those . . .)
    Pay (exchange of payment)
    Goods Handover (exchange of goods)
    Closing (exchange of thanks)
    Goodbye.

To native speakers the above structure may seem so obvious that it is not worthy of comment. We have learned the structure of such an exchange in childhood and we do not stop to think about the stages we go through to achieve our purchase goals. But if we were to find ourselves in a culture where buying and selling proceeded through bartering, and we had no previous experience of this, we would be at a loss. We would not know how to proceed. In the eyes of the natives of that culture it is likely that we would appear stupid. But our failure to handle bartering would not be an indication of lack of intelligence; it would be an indication of lack of experience within a certain culture. The point I am making is that the stages we go through in language to achieve our goals are social in origin. This is true of writing as well as speech. If we understand the sociocultural basis of the organisation of different types of texts we realise these structures are learned. They are not a reflection or manifestation of some innate ability; they are part of our sociocultural learning. If students do not read widely or well they are less likely to become familiar with the structure of some types of written texts. Yet we are likely to judge students' written texts that are inadequate in this respect as evidence of an intellectual failure of some kind. I would argue that such an approach is misguided as it fails to take account of the sociocultural basis of language use.

Report writing

Let us now look at two texts where there are marked differences in the handling of text structure. Both come from the same writing situation after a class excursion to the Applied Arts and Sciences Museum, as it then was. Text 3 was chosen by the class teacher as a successful one, while Text 4 was considered to be less successful.

The Year 6 class had been asked to write about the three things that interested them the most at the museum. In setting this topic for writing the teacher was aiming to move the students away from the type of writing which typically follows school excursions where the students write about one event after the other in the sequence in which they

Aplied Arts and Sciences Museum

At the museum a lot of things interested me but three things interested me the most they were the Planetarium, the Railway engines and the Mineral Wealth of Australia.

The Planetarium is a little room with a dome roof and a Planetarium Projector with lots of seats aroud the Projector. The way the projector works is it can show slides, photos of astronomy. The projector also shows the night sky with the stars, planet and moons of the planets. It can also move everything in the sky to where it would be in the sky.

My second choice was the Railway engines because I like trains and railways and I have a train set. The engines interested me because of the train noises the engines made I can't tell you how they work because I'm not sure.

My last choice was the Mineral Wealth of Australia because there was a board with a map of Australia on it and when you press the button of whatever you want to see wherever it is mined there will be a light there.

Applied Arts and sciences Museum

Clocks and swords

I like the Strasburg clock because it was a real clock and it was a good clock because it had the apostyles were moving around. The rooster started yelling coca-doda-do

SWORDS

I liked the swords because they were cold blunt some were sharp. they had the Uking sword and gun swords. they were dangrus. they had night swords too

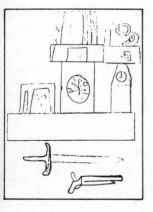

occurred. We are all familiar with the type of text that proceeds something like this:

First we saw the dinosaur skeletons. Then we saw the exhibits of Aboriginal weapons and tools. After that . . .

The teacher, through the wording of the task in this context, was giving the students a structure or pattern of organisation for their writing. It was a pattern which moved them towards report writing, which is about the way things are, and away from narrative writing, which is about what happens next.

In Text 3 there is a General Classification:

At the museum a lot of things interested me but three things interested me the most. They were the Planetarium, the Railway engines and the Mineral Wealth of Australia.

The General Classification is followed by Description. The three exhibits chosen by the writer as the ones he found most interesting are described. Note too, the writer's organisation of his text. After an introductory statement in which he names the three things he will write about he describes each in turn. He writes first about the Planetarium. The next exhibit he introduces with, *My second choice was . . .* and his third choice with, *My last choice was . . .*. This organisation is typical of factual writing where we first introduce what we are going to write about and then deal with a topic or argument, one by one, often using a numerical ordering of some kind.

Text 4 is very different from Text 3. The writer has chosen to write about the exhibits in terms of his personal reaction to them. He introduces each exhibit by saying *I liked . . .* This is followed by very brief observations about the things he has chosen to focus on. This type of writing has been identified by Martin and myself as Observation Comment. Our research has shown that it is a very common type amongst 'beginning writers'. In the first years of the infants' school young children commonly write observations regarding activities or events they have been involved in and comment about these in some way. We regard Observation Comment as an immature variety of writing. It does not occur in adult writing as a separate variety although elements of it may be found in long descriptions or in parts of a narrative. But the writer of this text was in Year 6 when it was written. He was about to enter secondary school with its array of writing demands, mainly of a factual kind in subjects apart from English. Any writer who is writing only, or mainly, Observation Comment texts will have great difficulty in meeting the demands of secondary school writing. Our research has shown that in each class in the primary school whose writing we collected throughout 1983 there were some children who wrote mainly this type of text in all writing situations. It seems to me it is a matter for considerable concern if a pupil after six years of schooling is still writing a variety that is immature and extremely limited in the goals it achieves.

You may say that the writer's personal response in Text 4 is still a worthwhile one; he is expressing his own reaction to what he saw and the text should be valued for this reason. I would agree with this but the writer's work needs to be considered in a wider context than that of individual response. It needs to be considered from the point of view of the writer achieving goals both in the school and the wider community. If the goal of a written text is to describe the way things are, then the Report is structured to do this, not the Observation Comment. If the writer of Text 4 continues to write an Observation Comment when a Report is asked for his writing will continue to be judged less successful than that of a writer who meets the demands of the task. Of course, as time goes by, the writer of Text 4 may learn to write Reports; he might 'catch on' to this type of writing but then again he might not. He has already been involved in many and varied language situations during his years at school. If he does not 'catch on' to the variety of writing appropriate to his task he will continue to limp along as far as writing is concerned. I would suggest, therefore, that teachers must be able to intervene where necessary to teach students the stages they need to go through in written language to achieve particular goals.

If we do not take up the challenge of teaching children to write we are accepting an inequitable education system as far as the development of writing abilities is concerned: one where the advantaged continue to be advantaged and the disadvantaged continue to be disadvantaged. The advantaged students are those who learn the strucures of texts largely on their own accord. They are not explicitly taught how to organise written texts but through their reading and patterns of interaction they develop mastery of a range of written varieties. The disadvantaged are those who, for a number of reasons, do not develop mastery of the ways written texts are organised to achieve goals. Included in this group are children learning English as a second language; children whose families are from a different culture; children who are poor readers; and children from certain socioeconomic groups in the community. If we do not teach these children to write we are denying them the opportunity for success in the education system.

Differences between speech and writing

There are other differences to be noted between Texts 3 and 4. Text 3, as we have noted, includes more information about the exhibits than Text 4. In Text 3 the writer introduces what he will write about and then describes each exhibit. The writer of Text 4 develops his text without any reference, apart from the title, to where he was or the purpose of his task. If you were not familiar with the Strasbourg clock written about in Text 4 you would find the text rather strange. Mention of a rooster and the apostles seems very strange and almost nonsensical in a text about a clock.

The two texts demonstrate fundamental differences between the spoken and written mode of language. In writing we are generally at a distance from the events and facts we write about and from our readers too. This distance exerts a pressure on our language to include more information in a text so that it can be as well understood as possible. In writing we create and re-create experience for a distant audience. The task is a difficult one; it is particularly demanding for school writers who write for a teacher who has either shared the experience they write about or is more of an expert in it than they are.

The writer of Text 3 handles the demands of the written mode well. Note the opening sentence of the second paragraph: *The Planetarium is a little room with a dome roof and a Planetarium Projector with lots of seats around the projector.* This description illustrates very well the writer's competence in re-creating experience for his audience, the teacher, as if he knows nothing of what was being written about.

Text 4 is more like language in the spoken mode. Indeed it is more like the language of face-to-face interaction. It could be part of an exchange such as the following:

Teacher: What did you like at the museum?
Student: I liked the Strasbourg clock.
Teacher: Why did you like that?
Student: Because it was a real clock, a good clock, etc. . . .

Text 4 does not give information about the setting nor much information about the exhibits. It assumes shared knowledge on the part of the reader of what is written about, hence the introduction of the apostles and the rooster without any prior explanation of their relationship with the clock. This writer has a great deal to learn about handling the written mode. One way of helping writers to perceive the need for more information in their writing is to give them the opportunity to write for audiences other than the teacher. I don't mean to imply that simply by introducing a new audience the problems of the written mode will be solved. The teacher needs to point out to writers, by reference to successful texts, what is needed in their writing if it is to successfully re-create an experience for someone who did not share it. The need to do this is likely to make more sense to the writer if the audience is genuinely a distant one.

Expository essays

Lastly I would like to consider an expository essay written by a Year 11 history student. The essay was written in Term 3 of the school year. The student had experienced difficulty with essay writing throughout the year. Her history essays were judged by her teacher to be generally weak, although it was apparent from her essays over the year that her writing had improved. Her teacher had worked with her to achieve this. Nevertheless her history writing still showed room for improvement.

Text 5
By the nineteenth century, the Manchu dynasty was on the verge of collapse; the West simply hastened its end. Discuss this statement with reference to the period between 1839 and 1911.

The power of the Manchu emperors, who had ruled China since the seventeenth century, was breaking down, and the central government could no longer maintain order and prevent corruption. The Chinese had become a backward people, ignorant of modern European knowledge and using medieval weapons in their futile attempts to keep out 'foreign devils'. Poverty was widespread because agricultural production, depending on primitive Chinese practice lagged behind population. Cholera, plague and other diseases ravished the land.

Because the dykes and other public works along the great rivers were neglected by the corrupt and inefficient government floods caused heavy loss of life and property. When . . . River changed its course to the great sea during a great flood in 1852, a huge area of rich agricultural land was swept away and millions of Chinese were left homeless. Thousands of destitute persons formed armed bands and added to the brigades which already had been spreading bloodshed and pillage throughout China.

The policy of isolation could not be maintained against the thrusting commercial activity of the nineteenth century. The first clash between China and Europe reflected no credit on Europe. In 1839 the Chinese government anxious to protect its people, forbade the importation of opium. The result was the so called Opium War, the first clash between China and a European power. By the treaty of Nanking (1892) which ended the way.

China was forced to pay large indemnity; Five ports (Canton, etc.) were opened for the British and so for all foreign trade. The British gained possession of the island of Hong Kong. British offenders against Chinese law were to be punished by British law under British authority, the first clear recognition of what we today call extraterritorality. In 1814 the United States secured similar privileges to those granted to Britain.

China had been troubled by foreign invasions. The Western powers had what was for them a satisfactory method of dealing with China. In 1856 the murder of a French missionary and the seizure of a Chinese vessel under the British flag provided Napoeon III with the excuse to wage a further war on China. This conflict became known as the second Opium War. Foreigners were allowed to travel inland, a large indemnity was again paid and six new ports were opened for trade. The importation of opium was legalised and Christian missionaries were guaranteed freedom.

European trade with China grew tremendously. There were no further wars between China and the Western powers in the closing quarter of the nineteenth century. Foreign influence within this ancient land steadily expanded, and the power of the Manchu dynasty steadily declined, before the end of the century it really seemed as if the 'opening up' of China would be its 'breaking up'.

The humiliating defeats inflicted on the imperial army and navy by small Anglo-French forces during the opium wars reduced the prestige of the Manchu government and affected its ability to suppress rebellions. Chinese sovereignty was weakened by extraterritorality and by the setting up of independent Christian communities within China.

Although Western powers artificially propped up the Manchu dynasty on some decisions Western impact strong enough to hasten downfall of Manchus by intensifying the weaknesses which were already apparent by the nineteenth century.

A major problem in this essay is that it lacks a Thesis of its own. There is a Thesis in the question:

By the nineteenth century, the Manchu dynasty was on the verge of collapse; the West simply hastened its end.

A successful essay, however, needs its own Thesis which is then defended or argued against by the writer. Without a Thesis it is difficult to develop a series of arguments supporting a case. You have no peg to hang your hat on so to speak. History teachers show an awareness of this when they make the comment, 'Your essay lacks a good introduction'. The teachers seem well aware that the success of an expository essay depends to a large extent on a successful introduction. I would suggest that 'introduction' is too general a term. It does not describe the particular function of the opening part of an essay. All essays have an introduction of some kind but the nature of the introduction varies according to the goal of the essay. In an expository essay the introduction is the Thesis of the essay. The Thesis may be largely a restatement of the Thesis in the question but it is usually developed or expanded in some way. Consider the opening of an essay from the same writing situation of Text 5 where the Thesis of the question is further developed.

> The Manchus invaded China in 1644 and overthrew the Ming dynasty. They set up the Ching dynasty, and ruled until 1912. However, what had been a period of stability for the Manchus had begun to decline rapidly in the 1800's. Years of rebellion followed which seriously weakened the Manchu power in China. The final collapse of the Ching dynasty was due partially from internal decay and partially from the steady increase of foreign pressure from the West and eventually from Japan.

After the Thesis comes the Argument in Exposition. In Text 5 the writer does not develop arguments to support a case but rather writes a Report about 'the way things were' in China during the Manchu period of rule. The reader can see the seeds of the arguments in the first two paragraphs. (For reasons of space and time I will restrict my comments to these two paragraphs only.) There is reference to the power of the emperors breaking down, the spread of corruption, poverty, disease, the neglect of public works, etc. But these facts are not turned into arguments; they are not related back to a Thesis; nor are they linked to the question as evidence of the impending breakdown of the Manchu dynasty.

In the second paragraph there is further evidence of the lack of argumentation. Consider, for example, the opening sentence:

> Because the dykes and other public works along the great rivers were neglected by the corrupt and inefficient government, floods caused heavy loss of life and property.

This paragraph is about the problems which stemmed from the inefficient government of the Manchus. What needs to be highlighted is that the corrupt and inefficient government was largely responsible for the social disorder of the period. But the fact that the government was *corrupt and inefficient* is tucked away in the middle of the sentence. It is not foregrounded as it needs to be at the beginning of the sentence where it would be the point of departure for the information of the sentence. The sentence would then read like this:

> The corrupt and inefficient government of the Manchus neglected public works including the maintenance of the dykes. As a result, when the floods came there was heavy loss of life and property.

This information needs to be foregrounded if an argument is to be developed to support the Thesis that the Manchu dynasty was on the verge of collapse. The other events depicted in this paragraph need also to be related to the inefficient government. For example, the writer implies, but does not make explicit, that the government could not cope with the consequences of the floods. Finally, all the information of the paragraph needs to be related to the Thesis so that it is clearly seen that because of the inefficient government many serious social and agricultural problems were not dealt with adequately by the Manchus, thus showing the government was on the verge of collapse. The writer has the information she needs for her purposes but she is not arguing as the essay demands. So often problems with essay writing are equated with problems of knowledge, lack of content and so forth. But this is not the case with this essay; nor is it, I suspect, with others. But the writer is not organising her resources to meet simultaneously the demands of the content of the question and the structure of the essay.

At this point you may object that I am putting the student and her meanings into some kind of strait-jacket by emphasising the structure of the essay. But this structure is not of my making; it is the structure of written argument in our society. It is indeed a type of constraint but it is one that is common to most of our language use in speech and writing. I do not think text structure inhibits a student's meaning. If we teach a student to handle the stages of Exposition we are teaching her to argue in the manner that is considered prestigious in our society. We are helping her to make her meanings effective. Those students who don't succeed in learning the stages of written varieties are, as I have already pointed out, at a disadvantage in the society. I could draw an analogy here between learning the structure of written varieties and learning the standard dialect of our community. In Australian communities Aborigines are one group who often speak a nonstandard variety of Australian English. For them learning the standard dialect is the means for effective participation in the community. It is a means for power. Aborigines working to secure a better place for their people within Australian society would scoff at the notion that they do not need to learn the standard dialect. They do not see the dialect as a constraint on meaning but a means for gaining power in the Australian community. Similarly, gaining control of writing strategies is a means for effective participation in educational contexts.

As writing is taught in our schools today there are serious contradictions. We reward essay writing that is structured appropriately but we do not make explicit our requirements for it. For those students who are able to handle the stages of different varieties of writing successfully the rewards come in high examination marks and university placements. For students who do not master the organisation of different varieties there is no success forthcoming in the education system. They receive low marks yet they are given little opportunity to master the structures of different texts. It is a strange situation that we know what we want in written work and reward it when we receive it but we do not let our students know in advance exactly what we are looking for. In other words we are operating within the framework of a hidden curriculum.

Teaching writing

It should by now be apparent that I am arguing strongly for teachers teaching writing where the students' needs are the main criteria rather than relying on development of writing abilities through a range of language experiences. So my last question is, what can teachers do to assist writers gain control of the structures of different types of texts?

I can only treat very briefly how teachers can intervene in writing development. Firstly, teachers should know what they require in writing in their subject as far as types of texts are concerned.

They should know the characteristics of the different types of texts asked for in their subject. This is a difficult requirement for teachers to meet at present as they are mostly working on a very implicit understanding of the structure of texts. But we must work towards making this implicit knowledge explicit if we are to break out of the hidden curriculum we now work within.

Secondly, we need to look at what our students read. Models for factual writing come mainly from text and reference books. If these are written badly we are providing students with poor models for writing. Books should be chosen or recommended with a view to the influence they can exert on student writing.

Thirdly, we should make use of our knowledge of text structures to make a positive assessment of students' writing wherever possible. We should look at writing in terms of the extent to which the text approximates the mature model of this variety. If we do this we can be positive and constructive in the comments we make. We are still bedevilled by an approach to essay writing which comments on the student's writing in terms of deficit. Because we lack an explicit model for text structure the only positive approach we can take at present is a very general one of encouragement. We are hard put to suggest strategies for the writer to follow to improve her writing.

Fourthly, if we make explicit what is involved in different types of writing we can plan to work on these in stages. For example, we can concentrate on developing a satisfactory Thesis as a distinct part of the essay. It may well be that the conference approach of Donald Graves could be employed to good effect here. It could be worthwhile to use the approach with teaching essay writing. One of my major criticisms of Graves' work, as it now stands, is that teachers are still working intuitively on the basis of implicit knowledge of texts so that the hidden curriculum still prevails.

I would be interested to see the method in action with teachers working on the basis of explicit knowledge of the structure of different types of texts. We should also make as much use as possible of successful writing by students to demonstrate how an essay is developed.

Finally, I think we should seriously consider teaching senior students the structures of the texts we ask them to write. At this stage explicit teaching related to their own writing and reading is likely to be both interesting and helpful.

Acknowledgements

I would like to thank Robyn Magennis of Bankstown Girls' High School, Patricia Warren of Marrickville High School and Helen Willis of North Sydney Girls' High School who, at very short notice, collected essay writing for me. I am most grateful to them for their assistance.

References

Brice Heath, S., *Ways with Words: Language, Life and Work in Communities and Classrooms* (Cambridge University Press, Cambridge, 1983).

Christie, F., *The 'received tradition' of English language study in schools: The decline of rhetoric and the corruption of grammar.* (Unpublished MA thesis, University of Sydney, 1981).

Christie, F., *Young children's writing development: The relationship of written genres to curriculum genres.* Paper given at the Conference on Language in Education, held at the Brisbane College of Advanced Education, Brisbane, 20–23 August, 1984.

Halliday, M.A.K., *Learning How to Mean: Exploration in the Development of Language* (Edward Arnold, London, 1975).

Halliday, M.A.K., *An Introduction to Functional Grammar* (Edward Arnold, London, 1985).

Hasan, R., 'Text in the systemic-functional model', in W. Dressler (ed.), *Current Trends in Text Linguistics*, Research in Text Theory (de Gruyter, Berlin, 1977).

Hasan, R., 'On the notion of text', in J.S. Petofi (ed.), *Text vs. Sentence* (Buske, Hamburg, 1979).

Kohl, H., *Reading, How to* (Penguin Education, Harmondsworth, 1974).

Kress, G., *Learning to Write* (Routledge & Kegan Paul, London, 1982).

Labov, W., & Waletzky, H., 'Narrative analysis: Oral versions of personal experience', in J. Helm (ed.), *Essays on the Verbal and Visual Arts* (University of Washington Press, Seattle, 1967), pp. 12–44.

Martin, J.R., & Rothery, J., *Writing Project Reports Numbers 1 and 2* (Department of Linguistics, Sydney University, 1980 & 1981).

Martin, J.R., 'Language, register and genre', in *Children Writing: Reader*, ECT418 Language Studies (Deakin University, Geelong, Victoria, 1984) pp. 21–30.

Rothery, J., 'The development of genres—primary to junior secondary school', in *Children Writing: Study Guide*, ECT418 Language Studies (Deakin University, Geelong, Victoria, 1984) pp. 67–114.

Ventola, E., *Contrasting Schematic Structures in Service Encounters* (Mimeo, University of Sydney, 1982).

Ventola, E., *The Structure of Social Interaction: a systemic approach to the semiotics of service encounters* (Pinter, London, 1987).

Reading 2

Exposition: literary criticism

J. R. Martin

The text

The Exposition to be considered was written by a female Year 11 student in a secondary girls' school on Sydney's north shore. The school admits students on the basis of high academic achievement in the primary school. It was written in response to an examination question which appears below. It can be seen from the marking scheme and the time available that had the student planned her time carefully, she would have produced the Exposition in about 25 minutes. The text produced was a successful one, highly valued in this situation type, and was accordingly awarded a high mark.

Source: J.R. Martin, 'Exposition: Literary criticism', in *Writing Report 1980* (Working Papers in Linguistics 1), Department of Linguistics, University of Sydney, Sydney, 1980, pp.4–22, 31–3.

The question

Time allowed: 2 hours
Marks: Chaucer   — 20
            Novel   — 40
            Drama   — 40

Section A
Chaucer
'There was also a Nonne, a Prioresse,
That of hir smylyng was ful symple and coy.
Hir gretteste ooth was but by Seint Loy;
And she was cleped Madame Eglentyne.
Ful wel she soong the service dyvyne,
Entuned in hir nose ful semely;
And Frenssh she spak ful faire and fetishly,
After the scole of Stratford atte Bowe,
For Frenssh of Parys was to hire unknowe.
At Mete wel ytaught was she with alle:
She leet no morsel from hir lippes falle,
Ne wette hir fyngres in hir sauce depe;'

'The Prioresse is created with considerable skill and we enjoy the mocking and humorous tone and comments.' Discuss how Chaucer has used the language of poetry to create these reactions. (Include rhythms, grammatical structures, sounds, alliteration, assonance, choice or words etc. etc.)

The question asked is a relatively clear one, not too open-ended. It presents a fairly straight-forward thesis to be discussed and even includes some 'tips' on what to mention in the answer. The text to be criticised is presented as part of the question. Both the wording of the question and the presence of the passage to be criticised influence the structure of the exposition in ways which will be discussed below.

The student's answer is presented below. Her spelling, 'grammar', and paragraphing have all been maintained. The text has been divided into units appropriate to the analysis presented in section 3. These units will be discussed at that time.

The answer

[1]Chaucer has used the language of poetry to create a mocking and humerous picture of the Nonne. [2]Chaucer first describes the Nonne by her facial expression. [3]He tells us that her smile was symple and coy, very sweet and lovely [3b]then mentioned that she took the oath by Saint Loy and was known as Madame Eglentyne. [4]It seems that Chaucer has deliberately used Eglentyne [4b]so that we might think of 'elegance' [5]for as the passage continues [5b]it is obvious that the Nonne is a very elegant women of the court.

[6]Chaucer now tells us of how well she sung the devine service, very elegantly and properly [7]but the next line 'Entuned in hir nose ful semely' seems to, by the words Chauce has chosen, drown any attempt at elegance. [8]Chaucer has used very nasal sounds in this line [8b]as though she sings through her nose and not clearly.

[9]'And Frenssh she spak ful faire and fetishly'. [10]Here Chaucer has used alliteration to empathsize the fact that the Nonne spoke French fairly well after the school at Bowe. [11]This is really not an accomplishment that a priorese must possess [12]yet Chaucer seems to think that it is important to stress this line using alliteration. [13]Chaucer is portraying to us a Nun of his time [13b]and is gently mocking the character of all nuns.

[14]'For Frenssh of Parys was to hire unknowe' is the next line.

[15]Chaucer has used sentence inversion in this line. [16]Instead of saying, the Nonne did not know the French of Paris [16b]he has expressed it as, For the French of Paris was to her unknow. [17]This is to keep the rythming even [17b]but also to stress that even though she can speak French from school, she is not a travelled woman and has never been to Paris though, of course, she wishes to give the impression of being elegant and courtly.

[18]At meals she always ate well and carefully, [19]she never let a morsel drop from her lips onto her dress [19b]and never let her fingers get wet [19c]when she dipped her food into the sauce bowl. [20]In fact she ate very genteely, like a lady.

[21]The passage consists of rythming couplets except for the first and last lines [22]and this is to stress the point of elegance in poetic form.

[23]Chaucer has presented to us a prioresse [24]but the irony of the passage is that he has told us nothing of her Christian duties, but only of her physical features and elegance. [25]He has stressed the point that she spoke French which is again connected with her elegance for it was the French who introduced the manners

and courtly ways of the French court into the English court. [26]He has told she ate gracefully and carefully and that the Nonne sang well [27]but this does not mean she was a good prioresse. [28]Chaucer is mocking the nuns of his time [29]for they are not devoutly religious [29b]but trying to be elegant women respected for their courtly ways and manners.

The analyses

In this section the text under consideration will be related to the linguistic system from which it derives in four ways: via lexical cohesion, schematic structure, conjunction, and theme. For each of these analyses, the systems involved will be briefly outlined. Then the structures generated by these systems in the text will be considered. Lexical cohesion will be considered first as its presentation helps to focus attention on what the essay is about. Much of the theoretical background to the analyses presented is found in Gleason (1968) and Halliday and Hasan (1976).

Lexical cohesion

System

Lexical cohesion has to do with 'relevance' in a text. Being relevant means staying on topic, moving from one idea to the next. To achieve this writers make use of expectancies readers have about what kinds of words go together. The technical term for these probabilities of cooccurrence is 'collocation'.

The associations that people make between words are based largely upon the taxonomic organisation of vocabulary in language. These taxonomies are based on subclassification ('a rose is a flower is a plant', etc.) and on part/whole relations ('a house has a door has a knob', etc.). In addition to associations between words that are close together in taxonomic terms, writers make use of collocational relations that are hard to define comprehensively (e.g. attributive relations such as 'dark' and 'night'; implicational relations such as 'husband' and 'marriage'; expectancy relations such as 'trip' and 'fall' and so on). The kinds of association sketched out here are presented as a system of choices in Figure 1. These options comprise the meaning potential underlying lexical cohesion in text within a model of language that treats meaning not as a 'thing' but as **choice**. Language is being treated here as a system that makes meanings (not as a system that turns meaning or thinking into sound).

Structure

An analysis of lexical cohesion in the Chaucer essay is presented in Figure 2. The principal lexical strings can be glossed as relating to 'literary criticism', 'what Chaucer does', 'the nun's appearance', 'elegance', 'religion', 'the text itself', 'singing', 'French', and 'eating'. These strings are of course sensitive to the fact that this text has as a part of its field another text. Thus certain of the strings relate to literary criticism, the fild of the text as a whole: 'literary criticism', 'what Chaucer

Figure 1   Lexical cohesion: the system

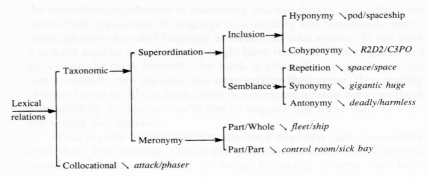

does', and 'the text itself'. Other strings relate to the field of Chaucer's text: 'religion', 'the nun's appearance', 'French', 'singing', and 'eating'. The 'elegance' string seems an interpretative one, bridging between the two fields. Note that the literary criticism strings tend to run through the text while strings relating to the field of Chaucer's text tend to cluster by paragraph. Paragraph 1 for example is concerned with the nun's appearance, paragraph 2 with her singing, 5 with her eating, and so on. And interestingly enough the concluding paragraph picks up all the text's strings, even those having only a very localised realisation elsewhere in the text.

The lexical structure of the essay is such that even before considering conjunction and theme the overall structure of the essay can be outlined. So the next section will deal with schematic structure.

Schematic structure

System

The term schematic structure refers to the beginning, middle, and end structure of texts. All texts have some kind of beginning, middle, and end though the exact nature of this organisation depends on genre. In narrative as we know it, where the purpose of the text is to tell a story, texts begin with an Orientation which introduces participants and says something about where and when. Then follows a Complication, a sequence of actions leading up to a crisis. Then comes a Resolution which solves the crisis. And sometimes a Coda is added, commenting on the story as a whole (see Labov & Waletzky 1967).

In essays on the other hand, where the purpose is to develop an argument, one begins with an introduction, stating the thesis advanced. Then one moves on to the Body of the essay which consists of the the series of Arguments supporting the thesis. Finally a Conclusion is added which restates the thesis and sums up the arguments.

Language is used for so many different purposes and involves so many types of schematic structure that linguists do not yet understand the choices involved well enough to write a network for them. So the outline of schematic structure presented above will have to suffice. Note however that writers choose between different purposes just as they choose between types of word association or types of conjunction and

Figure 2   The Chaucer essay: lexical cohesion

	Literary criticism	What Chaucer does	The Nun's appearance	Elegance	Religion	The text	Singing	French	Eating
Introduction (1)	language poetry mocking humerous	use create							
Argument 1: (2−5)		describe tell mention use	Nonne face expression smile symple coy sweet lovely	elegance elegant court	Nonne woman	passage			
Argument 2: (6−8)	nasal sounds	tell choose use		elegantly properly elegant		line word line	sing sing		
Argument 3: (9−13)	alliteration alliteration	empathsize think stress portraying			Nonne prioresse Nun			French speak French	
Argument 4: (14−17)	sentence inversion rythming even	use say express stress		elegant courtly	Nonne woman	line line		French Paris French Paris French Paris French Paris	
Argument 5: (18−20)				genteely lady					meal eat morsel lips finger sauce bowl food
Argument 6: (20−21)	rythming couplet poetic form	stress		elegance		passage line			
Conclusion: (20−21)	irony mean mocking	present tell stress tell	physical feature	elegance elegance manners courtly court court gracefully carefully elegant courtly manners	prioresse Christian duty Nonne prioresse nuns devoutly religious	passage	sing	speak French French French English	eat

that the meaning potential relevant to schematic structure will have to be formalised eventually.

The Chaucer essay

The schematic structure of the Chaucer essay is made up of an Introduction, what looks like 6 Arguments, and what appears to be a Conclusion. The introduction and first Argument are presented in paragraph 1, the second, third, fourth, fifth (?), and sixth (?) Arguments in paragraphs 2, 3, 4, 5 and 6 respectively. And the Conclusion (?) is presented in paragraph 7.

In the Introduction the thesis implicated by the exam question is clearly articulated. The Arguments will have to be structured to show how Chaucer uses the language of poetry to create a mocking and humorous picture of the Nun. In order to achieve this an argument must present a use of the language of poetry and connect it with some particular aspect of the Nun it is used to mock. The first four Arguments of the essay in fact do this very well. Argument 1 relates the phonaesthesia of the Nun's name, Eglentyne, to her appearance. Argument 2 relates nasal sounds to her singing. Argument 3 relates alliteration to her French and Argument 4 relates sentence inversion to the same topic. It is interesting to note here that while the lexical string oriented to the field of Chaucer's text, the 'French' string, calls for a single paragraph, the lexical string oriented to the field of the text itself, 'literary criticism', points to two paragraphs since two distinct literary devices are introduced. For reasons having to do with conjunction, which will be discussed below, the latter paragraphing decision is employed. The schematic structure of the essay was included in Figure 2.

Arguments 5 and 6 are less successful and it may be that they should thus not be analysed as Arguments at all. Argument 5 refers to the Nun's eating habits but does not connect this to a literary device. Argument 6 on the other hand refers to the language of poetry, specifically rhythm, but fails to consider what aspect of the Nun rhythm is mocking. In these Arguments the balanced exemplification needed to support the thesis is missing.

The Conclusion as well must in fact be considered as something of a failure in that although it has the appearance of summing up the essay, which it achieves by picking up all of the essay's major lexical strings, it does not restate the thesis of the essay nor really sum up the arguments supporting the thesis. Reference is made to those aspects of the Nun's character Chaucer mocks: appearance, singing, French, and her eating. But no mention is made of the language of poetry used to do so: choice of the Nun's name, nasal sounds, alliteration, or sentence inversion. An alternative version of the Conclusion will be considered later.

This is perhaps the appropriate place to speculate upon the reasons for these weaknesses in the essay. First of all there is the question of time pressure. In 25 minutes not much can be done in the way of planning and revision. The student is forced simply to work through the passage given to be criticised, notice what she can, and react to things in the order Chaucer discusses them. The amount of time allowed thus imposes a kind of linearity on the argument that is somewhat inappropriate. Second there is the problem of taking the 'tips' given in parentheses in the question seriously. One can almost picture the student pausing after Argument 5 when she has worked through to the end of Chaucer's passage, looking back at the question, noting that she hasn't discussed rhythm yet, and putting it in. Were it not for time pressure the topic of Argument 5, the Nun's eating, could perhaps have been included in Argument 1 and connected to the phonaesthesia of the Nun's name. And Argument 6 might more appropriately have been placed in the introduction where a general statement about the relation of elegance to the rhythm of the poem as a whole could have been added as a generalised example of the thesis. The interaction between schematic structure and lexical cohesion discussed above is presented in Table 1.

Table 1   The interaction of lexical cohesion and schematic structure

	Language of poetry	mocking the nun
Introduction	language of poetry	mocking the nun
Argument 1	phonaesthesia	appearance
Argument 2	nasal sounds	singing
Argument 3	alliteration	French
Argument 4	sentence inversion	French
Argument 5	–	eating
Argument 6	rhythm	–
Conclusion	–	(all)

It would perhaps be remiss here not to sympathise with the sense of 'quiet desperation' a student must feel when faced with this type of question. Each of the first four Arguments is as it is presented patently absurd, though admittedly totally appropriate in this context. It is hard to see how phonaesthesia, nasal sounds, alliteration or sentence inversion can be causally connected to the mocking and humorous effect achieved. This is of course not the student's fault. She is 'playing the game' well as it has been structured for her. But how much easier her task might be if the richness of language as a resource for the creation of verbal art was taught in secondary school instead of being trivialised into a list of literary devices which are simply the generic icing on an intriguingly more sophisticated cake.

Again, in the student's defence, it should be pointed out that her Conclusion may not be as inappropriate as it seems given the model of literary criticism that underlies much secondary teaching, deriving from the work of Leavis. In this 'school' it is a subjectively empathetic 'response' that is crucial to interpretation. Perhaps by choosing to demonstrate her sensitivity to the 'meaning' of the passage in her Conclusion the student is producing a text more highly valued than one which replays a set of potentially embarrassing arguments predicated on the rather mundane interpretation of 'poetic language' implied in the question.

Conjunction

The system

Conjunction has to do with being logical, in the natural language sense of the term. This involves relating clauses to each other in a text in terms of time, cause, comparison, or addition. Temporal relations are those realised by conjunctions like *when*, *while*, *after*, *before*, *then*, etc. and can be divided into those which are successive and those which are simultaneous. These relations are very common in narrative. Consequent relations are realised through *because*, *if*, *although*, *so that*, *therefore*, etc. and can be subclassified as causal, conditional, concessive, and purposive. These relations are more important in argument than in narrative. Comparative relations are realised through *whereas*, *like*, *similarly*, etc. and mark relations of contrast or similarity between clauses. Additive relations are realised by *and*, and *or*, and either simply join clauses to a text or express alternatives.

One of the most crucial, though perhaps the most subtle, distinctions relating to conjunction is that between internal and external conjunction. External conjunction relates propositions about the world to each other. Internal conjunction relates speech acts to each other, making connections in what might be termed the rhetorical world of discourse. Consider the ambiguity in *John is here because I saw him*. On the external reading this relates two facts in the world, the speaker seeing John and his presence, as Cause and Effect. That is, the speaker perhaps saw John and told him to come. On the internal reading seeing John is not the cause of him coming. Instead the causal connection must be paraphrased along the lines of: *I just saw John and that's why I'm **telling** you he's here*. It is not that the speaker told John to come. Rather, justification is given for telling the listener that John is present. Almost all conjunctions can be used both internally and externally.

Two conjunctive relations which are important in essay writing and which are always internal have to do with internal comparative similarity, relations often signalled by the conjunctions *that is* and *for example* or the abbreviations *i.e.* and *e.g.* The i.e. relation involves restatement: two different ways of expressing the same fact. With the e.g. relation an example is given of a particular fact. This example, when it is an example in support of a thesis, often has an internal causal flavour (i.e. *the reason I made that statement/here is an example*). An example of an i.e. relation would be: *John is crazy. Like he's completely nuts*. Compare the e.g. relation which is in fact a non-exhaustive i.e.: *John is crazy. Like you should see him drive*.

Conjunctive relations may be either subordinating or nonsubordinating: *John left after Mary arrived* vs *Mary arrived. Then John left*. And they may be either explicit or implicit. Conjunctions stamp logical relations between clauses. They do not create them. Juxtaposition alone is enough to signal that clauses are conjunctively related. Thus *John came home. He had a beer* and *John came home. Then he had a beer.* are both related in terms of temporal succession. The first is simply more explicit than the second.

The meaning potential composed of these distinctions is outlined in Figure 3.

Structure

For purposes of analysing conjunctive relations, the Chaucer essay has been divided into clauses which have or could have had an explicit conjunction between them (into 'conjunctively relatable units' in other words). Relative clauses, facts, reports, and nominalised clauses functioning as Subject or Complement are thus not treated as separate units.

Figure 3   Conjunction: the system

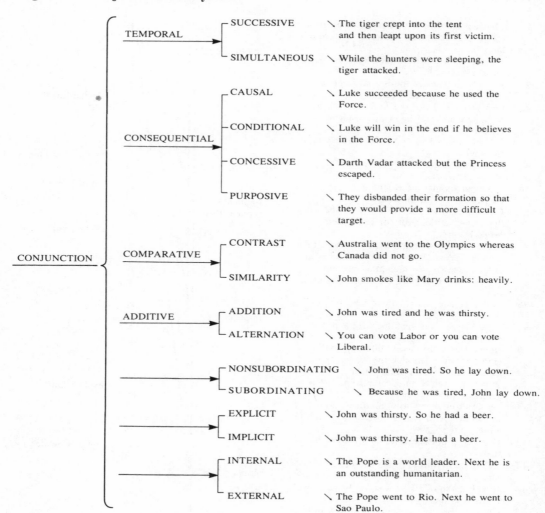

The conjunctive structure of the Chaucer essay is presented in Figure 4. Internal relations are represented down the left-hand side of the diagram, external relations down the right; except that external additives are modelled down the centre between units and all implicit additives are ignored. Each conjunctive relation is marked as explicit or implicit and according to logical type and the clauses the relation connects are joined by lines.

There is not space here to go into the analysis in detail. The most important relations to note are the four internal e.g. causal relations connecting 2—5b, 6—8b, 9—13b, and 14—17b to 1. The units 2—5b correspond to Argument 1, 6—8b to Argument 2, 9—13b to Argument 3, and 14—17b to Argument 4. Thus it can be seen that internal conjunction is interacting with lexical cohesion to realise the schematic structure of the essay. Arguments 5 and 6 which were perhaps intended as further examples fail and so are not connected to 1 in the diagram.

Figure 4   The Chaucer essay: conjunctive structure

1   Chaucer has used the language of poetry to create a mocking and humerous picture of the Nonne.

2   Chaucer first describes the Nonne by her facial expression.

3   He tells us that her smile was simple and coy, very sweet and lovely

3b   then mentioned that she took the oath by Saint Loy and was known as Madame Eglentyne.

4   It seems that Chaucer has deliberately used Eglentyne

4b   so that we might think of 'elegance'

5   for as the passage continues

5b   it is obvious that the Nonne is a very elegant woman of the court.

6   Chaucer now tells us of how well she sung the divine service, very elegantly and properly

7   but the next line 'Enturned in hir nose ful semely' seems to, by the words Chauce has chosen, drown any attempt at elegance.

8   Chaucer has used very nasal sounds in this line

8b   as though she sings through her nose and not clearly

9   'And Frenssh she spak ful faire and fetishly'

10   Here Chaucer has used alliteration to empathsize the fact that the Nonne spoke French fairly well after the school at Bowe

11   This is not really an accomplishment that a prioresse must possess

12   yet Chaucer seems to think that it is important to stress this line using alliteration.

13   Chaucer is portraying to us a Nun of his time

13b   and is gently mocking the character of all nuns.

14   'For Frenssh of Parys was to her unknowe' is the next line.

15   Chaucer has used sentence inversion in this line.

16   Instead of saying, the Nonne did not know the French of Paris

16b   He has expressed it as, For the French of Paris was to her unknow.

17   This is to keep the rythming even

17b   but also to stress that even though she can speak French from school, she is not a travelled woman and has never been to Paris though, of course, she wishes to give the impression of being elegant and courtly.

18   At meals she always ate well and carefully,

19   She never let a morsel drop from her lips onto her dress

19b   and never let her fingers get wet

19c   when she dipped them into the sauce bowl.

20   In fact she ate very genteely, like a lady.

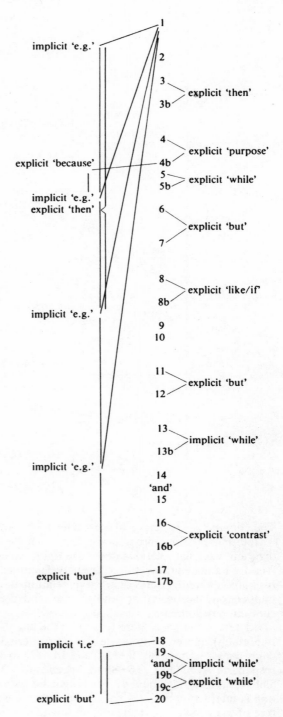

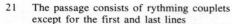

21	The passage consists of rythming couplets except for the first and last lines	21 'and'
22	and this is to stress the point of elegance in poetic form.	22
23	Chaucer has presented to us a picture of a prioresse	23
24	but the irony of the passage is that he has told us nothing of her Christian duties, but only of her physical features and elegance.	24
25	He has stressed the point that she spoke French which is again connected with her elegance for it was the French who introduced the manners and courtly ways of the French court into the English court.	25
26	He has told us that she ate gracefully and carefully and that the Nonne sang well	26
27	but this does not mean she was a good prioresse	27
28	Chaucer is mocking the nuns of his time	28
29	for they are not devoutly religious	29
29b	but trying to be elegant women respected for their courtly ways and manners.	29b

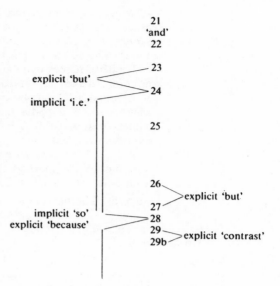

The second pattern worth noting is another internal one, relating 18 through 20 and 24 through 28. In both cases a fact is stated (in 18 and 24), restated (in 19—19c and 25—27 respectively), and then this restatement is linked via a consequential relation (via an explicit *but* to 20 and via an explicit *so* to 28) to the further statement. It is very common for a clause to be conjunctively related retrospectively to one unit and prospectively to another. When groups of clauses are related 'backwards' and 'forwards' in this way very tightly structured sandwich paragraphs result.

It is perhaps worth commenting at this point that conjunction can be fairly straight forwardly analysed in a 'good' essay. But in 'poor' writing the links are often so opaque as to be uninterpretable. Conversely, and the reasons for this are unclear, we have found that lexical cohesion is easier to analyse in a poor essay than in a good one. This presumably has something to do with a more complex associational development in good writing. But this requires further research.

Theme

The system

Theme has to do with the particular angle one takes on the content of a text in its development. Theme is realised in English by putting the clause constituent which takes part in this development first. Thus the 'point of departure' of English clauses reflects discourse patterns relevant to the structure of paragraphs and essays as a whole (see Fries 1978).

In English text, where the text is reflective, constructing experience, clauses commonly begin with a Textual Theme relating the clause conjunctively to what has gone before. This may be followed by an Interpersonal Theme expressing the writer's attitude to what he is saying. Then follows a Topical Theme realising that aspect of the field of the text which has been selected as its method of development. In the sentence *But frankly such training is often irrelevant to the needs of teachers in the classroom, but* is the Textual Theme; *frankly*, the Interpersonal Theme; and *such training*, the Topical Theme.

Topical Themes may be either marked or unmarked depending on how common and easy it is for a clause constituent to come first. English is a so-called SVO language where the Subject typically comes first in declaratives and encodes the content of an unmarked Theme. When Adjuncts (e.g. *in the classroom* in *In the classroom such training is often irrelevant.*) and less commonly Complements (e.g. *what teachers need to know* in *What teachers need to know this college doesn't teach*) come before the Subject marked Themes are realised. The choices sketched out here are presented in Figure 5.

Figure 5   Theme: the system

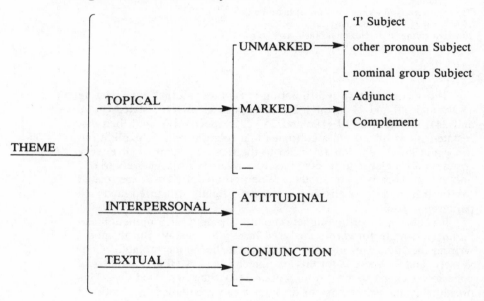

It needs mentioning here in light of a common prescriptive practice in the teaching of writing cautioning against the use of the passive that one of the functions of passive in English is to make a constituent an unmarked Theme. For example in *What teachers need to know isn't taught by this college, what teachers need to know* is unmarked Theme instead of marked Theme as in the example given above (cf. *this college* as unmarked Theme in the active: *This college doesn't teach what teachers need to know*). For a teacher to caution a student against the use of the passive can thus be seen as denying him a part of the potential present in English for producing coherent text, and reflects complete ignorance of the function of this text forming resource in English.

Structure

For the purposes of analysing theme, the same units have been used as for the conjunction analysis except that subordinate adverbial clauses (4b, 5, 8b, 16 and 19c) and clauses in branched paratactic structures involving Subject ellipsis (3b, 13b, 17b, 19b and 29b) are not treated as separate units. This is because adverbial clauses function as Theme themselves in units like 5 and the unmarked Theme of the second clause in branched structures like 3 is elliptical. The Theme analysis of the text is presented in Figure 6.

Figure 6   The Chaucer essay: thematic structure

Theme	Rheme. . .
1 *Chaucer*	has used the language of poetry to create a mocking and humerous picture of the Nonne.
2 *Chaucer*	first describes the Nonne by her facial expression.
3 *He*	tells us that her smile was symple and coy, very sweet and lovely then mentioned that she took the oath by Saint Loy and was known as Madame Eglentyne.
4 *It seems that Chaucer*	has deliberately used Eglentyne so that we might think of 'elegance'
5 *for as the passage continues*	it is obvious that the Nonne is a very elegant woman of the court.
6 *Chaucer*	now tells us of how well she sung the devine service, very elegantly and properly
7 *but the next line 'Entuned in hir nose ful semely'*	seems to, by the words Chauce has chosen, drown any attempt at elegance.
8 *Chaucer*	has used very nasal sounds in this line as though she sings through her nose and not clearly. 'And Frenssh she spak ful faire and fetishly'
9 *Here*	Chaucer has used alliteration to empathsise the fact that the Nonne spoke French fairly well after the school at Bowe.
10 *This*	is really not an accomplishment that a prioresse must possess.
11 *Yet Chaucer*	seems to think that it is important to stress this line using alliteration.
12 *Chaucer*	is portraying to us a Nun of his time and is gently mocking the character of all nuns.
13 *'For Frenssh of Parys was to hire unknowe'*	is the next line.
14 *Chaucer*	has used sentence inversion in this line.
15 *Instead of saying, the Nonne did not know the French of Paris*	he has expressed as, For the French of Paris was to her unknow.
16 *This*	is to keep the rythming even but also to stress that even though she can speak French from school, she is not a travelled woman and has never been to Paris though, of course, she wishes to give the impression of being elegant and courtly.

17 *At meals*	she always ate well and carefully,
18 *she*	never let a morsel drop from her lips onto her dress and never let her fingers get wet when she dipped them into the sauce bowl.
19 *In fact she*	ate very genteely, like a lady.
20 *The passage*	consists of rythming couplets except for the first and last lines
21 *and this*	is to stress the point of elegance in poetic form.
22 *Chaucer*	has presented to us a prioresse
23 *but the irony of the passage*	is that he has told us nothing of her Christian duties, but only of her physical features and elegance.
24 *He*	has stressed the point that she spoke French which is again connected with her elegance for it was the French who introduced the manners and courtly ways of the French court into the English court.
25 *He*	has told us that she ate gracefully and carefully and that the Nonne sang well
26 *but this*	does not mean she was a good prioresse
27 *Chaucer*	is mocking the nuns of his time.
28 *for they*	are not devoutly religious but trying to be elegant women respected for their courtly ways and manners.

The best way to appreciate the significance of Theme in a particular text is to consider alternative points of departure for clauses in the text. In the Chaucer essay there are perhaps three main candidates which might have been selected as a method of development: Chaucer, literary criticism, or the nun (the latter being in fact the method of development of this part of Chaucer's prologue). Clearly it is Chaucer that has been selected in the text examined here. Just under half the Topical Themes refer to Chaucer, many more than for any other aspect of the field. Just why Chaucer has been selected is uncertain. The student may have been influenced by the wording of the question which when reworded as a thesis has Chaucer as Theme (i.e. *Chaucer has used the language of poetry to . . .*). Or it may well be that generic factors are involved. In narrative, a genre more familiar to students in their oral, written, and previous writing experience, persons (in the form of heroes and heroines) function as the method of development of the story. So it may be that selecting Chaucer as the point of departure for so many clauses has the student using a pattern from the more familiar genre as a kind of bridge into expository writing. The time pressure under which the essay was written adds plausibility to this speculation.

Whatever the reasons for selecting Chaucer as Theme, it is worth considering the alternative more appropriate to the genre literary criticism. On the basis of the analysis of lexical cohesion and conjunction presented above, the following version of the last paragraph was constructed in an attempt to include reference to the language of poetry in the Conclusion:

96

In this passage Chaucer has used a number of poetic devices to present an ironic picture of nuns in his time.

His choice of the nun's name, Eglentyne, stresses her elegance.

Assonance underlines the haughty yet overly nasal nature of her singing.

Alliteration and sentence inversion are used to emphasise how non-Parisian her French was.

And the metre of the passage as a whole accords well with the nun's elegance.

In this way Chaucer skillfully manipulates the language of poetry to expose the nuns of his time for what they were.

This rewritten version was done naively as far as Theme analysis is concerned. But it was interesting to note, some months later when Theme was considered, that the rewritten version had in fact selected literary criticism as its method of development. Four out of the final six Themes in the text refer to the language of poetry. Linguistically naive readers of this version have pointed out that although it is a better summary of the argument of the essay, it does not fit into the essay. And the reason for this is of course that its method of development clashes with that of the student's essay. Note in passing that Arguments 5 and 6, analysed above as failing in the text, also depart from the method of development of the text. Argument 5 takes the Nun as its method of development and the Themes in Argument 6 simply refer to the passage and then to facts about it.

Before attempting to relate the patterns described above to expository and other types of writing in the next section, their relation to paragraphing will be considered. In principle, in exposition paragraphs tend to reflect the schematic structure of a text. Boundaries between paragraphs are thus realised through an interaction of conjunction, lexical cohesion, and theme. At times two or more of these patterns may pull in different directions. For example Arguments 3 and 4 in the Chaucer essay have a lot of lexical cohesion in common, oriented as they are to the Nun's French. But since both arguments stand in an e.g. relation to the same clause and since this e.g. relation is closely connected to the schematic structure of the text, the student uses two paragraphs instead of one. Another conflict arises with the Introduction, which in terms of conjunction and schematic structure should perhaps be a separate paragraph. But its length mitigates against this and since it is lexically and thematically related to the clauses which follow it is included in the first paragraph. What this discussion indicates is that paragraphs cannot be defined in a categorical way and that some kind of probabilistic model for discourse structure, deriving perhaps from variation theory, will be needed in future research.

References

Barnes, D., 'Review of *Language in Education: Language Development Project, Phase 1*', in J.Maling-Keepes & B.D. Keepes (eds.), *British Journal of Curriculum Studies* **12** (3), 1980, pp. 227–79.

Britton, J., *Language and Learning* (Pelican Books, Harmondsworth, 1972).

Britton, J., Burgess, T., Martin, N., McLeod, A., & Rosen, H., *The Development of Writing Abilities (11–18)* (Schools Council and Macmillan, London, 1975).

Christie, F., *The teaching of English in elementary schools in NSW, 1848–1900: An enquiry into social conditions and pedagogical theories determining the teaching of English* (Unpublished thesis, University of Sydney, 1976).

Christie, F., & Rothery, J., 'English in Australia: An interpretation of role in curriculum', in J. Maling-Keepes & B.D. Keepes (eds.), *Language in Education: Language Development Project, Phase 1* (Curriculum Development Centre, Canberra, 1979), pp. 197–242.

Christie, F., & Rothery J., *Language in Teacher Education: Child Language Development and English Language Studies*, Occasional Papers 3 (Applied Linguistics Association of Australia, Sydney, 1979).

Dixon, J., *Growth through English* (National Association for the Teaching of English and University Press, Oxford, 1967).

Fries, P., The status of theme in English (Department of Linguistics, University of Sydney, Mimeo, 1978).

Gleason, H.A., 'Contrastive analysis and discourse structure', in J.E. Alatis (ed.), *Report of the 19th Annual Round Table Meeting on Linguistics and Language Studies*, Georgetown Monograph Series on Language and Linguistics 21 (Georgetown University Press, Washington, DC, 1968), pp. 39–63. Reprinted in A. Makkai & D. Lockwood (eds.), *Readings in Stratificational Linguistics* (University of Alabama Press, Alabama, 1973), pp. 258–76.

Gregory, M., 'A theory for stylistics—exemplified: Donne's "Holy Sonnet XIV"', *Language and Style* **22** (2), 1974, pp. 108–18.

Halliday, M.A.K., 'Linguistic function and literary style: An enquiry into the language of William Golding's *The Inheritors*', in S. Chatman (ed.), *Literary Style: A Symposium* (Oxford University Press, New York, pp. 362–400, 1971). Reprinted in M.A.K. Halliday, *Exploration in the Functions of Language* (Edward Arnold, London, 1973), pp. 103–43.

Halliday, M.A.K., 'The functional basis of language', in *Explorations in the Functions of Language* (Edward Arnold, London, 1973), pp. 22–45.

Halliday, M.A.K., *Language and Social Man*, Schools Council Programme in Linguistics and English Teaching: Papers, Series 2, vol. 3 (Longman, London, 1974).

Halliday, M.A.K., *Learning How to Mean: Explorations in the Development of Language,* Explorations in Language Study (Edward Arnold, London, 1975).

Halliday, M.A.K., 'Text as semantic choice in social contexts', in T.A. Van Dijk & J. Petofi (eds.), *Grammars and Descriptions*, Research in Text Theory (De Gruyter, Berlin and New York, 1977).

Halliday, M.A.K., & Hasan, R., *Cohesion in English*, English Language Series 9 (Longman, London, 1976).

Harris, R.J., *An Experimental Inquiry into the Functions and Value of Formal Grammar in the Teaching of English with Special Reference to the Teaching of Correct Written English to Children Aged Twelve to Fourteen* (Unpublished PhD thesis, University of London, 1962).

Hasan, R., 'Rime and reason in literature', in S.Chatman (ed.), *Literary Style: A Symposium* (Oxford University Press, New York, 1971), pp. 229–326.

Hasan, R., 'The place of stylistics in the study of verbal art', *Skriptor*, 1975, pp. 49–62.

Hasan, R., 'Text in the systemic functional model', in W.U. Dressler (ed.), *Current Trends in Text Linguistics*, Research in Text Theory 2 (De Gruyter, Berlin, 1977), pp. 228–46.

Keen, J., *Teaching English: A Linguistic Approach* (Methuen, London, 1978).

Labov, W., & Waletzky, J., 'Narrative analysis: Oral versions of personal experience', in J.Helm (ed.), *Essays on the Verbal and Visual Arts*, Proceeding of the 1966 Annual Spring Meeting of the American Ethnological Society (University of Washington Press, Seattle, 1967), pp. 12–44.

Loban, W., *Language Development: Kindergarten through Grade Twelve*, NCTE Research Report No. 18 (National Council of Teachers of English, Champaign, Il, 1976).

Mackay, D., Thompson, B., & Schaub, P., *Breakthrough to Literacy: Teacher's Manual* (Longman, London, 1970).

Mellon, J.C., *Transformational Sentence-combining: A Method for Introducing Fluency in English composition*, NCTE Research Report No. 10 (National Council of Teachers of English, Champaign, Ill, 1969).

Strunk, W., & White, E.B., *The Elements of Style*, rev. edn (Macmillan, New York, 1959).

The Bullock Report, *A Language for Life* (HMSO, London, 1975).

Thornton, G., *Teaching Writing: The Development of Written Language Skills*, Explorations in Language Study (Edward Arnold, London, 1980).

Wardaugh, R., 'Ability in written composition and transformational grammar', *Journal of Educational Research* **60**(9), 1967.

Watson, K.D., *The new English in New South Wales secondary schools: A study of the origins and implementation of the 1971 English syllabus (years 7–10) with implications for future curriculum development* (Unpublished thesis, University of Sydney, 1978).

Technical terms

Acknowledgements

Grateful acknowledgement is made to the following sources for material used in this book.

p.22, extract from J. Carr, W. Murphy & I. Kindt, *In a Manner of Speaking: Teacher Notes and Suggested Activities*, Curriculum Services Branch, Department of Education, Brisbane, 1984, pp. 17–18.

pp. 38–9, extract which first appeared in 'Habitat Australia', colour magazine of the Australian Conservation Foundation.

Reading 1: J. Rothery, Writing to learn and learning to write. Paper delivered to an Inservice Study Day for the NSW Department of Education, Sydney, 1985, pp. 9–26, 27, 28–9.

Reading 2: J. R. Martin, 'Exposition: Literary criticism', in *Writing Report 1980* (Working Papers in Linguistics), Department of Linguistics, University of Sydney, Sydney, 1980, pp. 4–22, 31–3.

DATE DUE

MR 15 '91			

HIGHSMITH   #LO-45102